The Collectible Dionne Quintuplets

And Their Life Story

ANNETTE   CECILE   DR.A.R.DAFOE   MARIE   YVONNE   EMILIE

Other Books by the Author
Collectible Boy Dolls
Collectible Dolls in National Costume

The Collectible
Dionne Quintuplets

by John Axe

Published By HOBBY HOUSE PRESS
Riverdale, Maryland 20840

Additonal Copies Available $14.95 from:
HOBBY HOUSE PRESS
4701 Queensbury Road
Riverdale, Maryland 20840
or available from your favorite bookstore

Printed in the United States of America
ISBN: 0-87588-136-X

Dedicated
To
The Memory Of

Katharine Griswold Clark
Who was everything that she should have been—And More.

Acknowledgements

My goal has been to present a unique aspect of popular history, based on the principles of historical research and the analytical process. This could not have been done without the cooperation and the support of a great many individuals whom I am privileged to call my friends.

I particularly wish to convey my gratitude to the following persons without whom I could not have completed the project:

For their valuable aid and for their professional capacity—Betty Lamorie, the Librarian of *The North Bay Nugget*; Ann Przelomski, the Managing Editor of the *Youngstown Vindicator*, the Reference Librarians of the Public Library of Youngstown and Mahoning County; the Reference Librarians of the Columbus Public Library; and the Reference Librarians of the Metropolitan Toronto Library Board.

For their time and for the information they availed to me—Mr. and Mrs. Stan Guignard of the Dionne Quints Homestead Museum in North Bay, Ontario.

For their assistance with technical aspects— my sister, Bette Ann Axe; Kay Bransky; C. Kenneth Clark, Jr.; Susan Fogaras, Christine Kelly and Dr. Lowell Satre of the History Department of Youngstown State University; Phyllis Houston; Shirley and James Olson; Ted Tarr; Loretta Zablotny; and Paul Zimmerman.

For their graciousness and unprecedented generosity in permitting me to come into their homes with photographic equipment and for trusting me with their valuable collections—Lorene Anderson; Lois Barrett; Betty Cataldo; Connie Chase; Barbara DeVault; Wanda Lodwick; Marge Meisinger; Jimmy and Fay Rodolfos; Donna Stanley, the Editor of *Collectors United;* and Mary Stuecher. The willingness of these collectors to share their treasures is what collecting is all about.

And for all that she has done for me—I am deeply indebted to Patricia R. Smith, the author of *Modern Collector's Dolls*.

Table Of Contents

Introduction

My memory of the Dionne Quintuplets begins with what we called the "By-Owny Twin Spoons." The spoons had been around for a long time before my sister and I had decided that we could not eat off any other utensil except the spoons representing these celebrated persons, of whom we knew nothing but that there were five of them who were alike. During a summer, at the height of this fad, it was even worse. Our cousin came to visit and immediately developed the same affinity. She too would not let a morsel pass to her mouth unless it was from a "By-Owny Twin Spoon." And the spoon from which each ate *had* to be a certain spoon. The certain spoon would change from time to time and all three would insist that they wanted Emilie, for example. If one had captured Emilie, Yvonne or Marie would not do for either of the other two. To restore order, dry tears and feed the three capricious diners, the "By-Owny Twin Spoons" were publicly and ceremoniously dumped into the garbage can and forbidden to be rescued.

But this memory from early childhood, seen in a different light now, is one of the ingredients for contributing to my becoming a collector years later. My interest in the Dionnes came back after a friend told me that he remembered visiting the Quints as a child and a collector friend gave me her original newspaper about their birth. Any collection is just the beginning of what the hobby really is and there is no end to it. Over the years I came across newspaper items referring to a death or a birthday of the Dionnes, never learning much about their early years. Since 1934 there have been hundreds, if not thousands, of different articles manufactured to represent the Quintuplets. The most collectible are probably the dolls produced by the Alexander Doll Company, but all the other items supplement and enhance a Dionne collection. Finding new things is what makes collecting exciting. All these collectibles represent five very famous Canadian sisters. Although a collector could become too enamored of the individuals who are the subject of the collection, and make the mistake of thinking that the collections are religious relics of the admired one, it is interesting to learn about those persons who are the root of the collection, follow their experiences and vicariously share the limelight with them. Collectors are not "fans." Fans devote their energy to admiring an individual. Collectors are "buffs" who want to know every single detail about the persons who inspired the collectibles, and even more information about the collectibles themselves.

The fascinating hobby of collecting is probably not beneficial to humanity but in its own way it can enrich one's life and provide constructive entertainment, at the same time preserving aspects and artifacts of the past. We could speculate about all the purposes of collecting and perhaps psychoanalyze collectors and find many divergent reasons for their desire to collect, from it being sublimination for some lack in their lives to an inordinate desire to possess material goods. Collecting could even be a highly peculiar form of insanity. Valid as all these reasons may be, the person who is a collector does not care and will always notice one inevitabel result:

It is a lot of fun.

On the road leading to where the Dionne Quintuplets were born, Callander, Canada.—4.

Illustration 1. Old postcard from Callander.

Illustration 2. The Dionne home in 1934.

I. There Were Five Of Them
And They Were All Alike

In October of 1934, the Long March by the Chinese Communists began. Mao Tse-tung led 100,000 people in a 6,000 mile trek from the south to the north of China. Only 20,000 completed the journey to reach Yenan a year later. On August 2, 1934, President von Hindenburg of Germany died. Adolph Hitler then consolidated the offices of President and Chancellor and became Fuerher. Before these historic developments of 1934 had occurred, on May 28 in Corbeil, Ontario, the Dionne Quintuplets, the first set to survive unbroken beyond fifty minutes, were born. They are still the only *identical* set ever to survive. This third event, though it did not have world political importance as did the other two, received more press coverage and international attention because people could relate to it personally.

The Dionne Quintuplets were marketed as a saleable commodity from the beginning. A farm two miles east of the village of Callander and halfway to the hamlet of Corbeil in northern Ontario was the site of a five ring circus that played for several years. North Bay, nine miles to the north of Callander, and also on Lake Nipissing, was the only town of any size in the region, having a population of about 15,000 in 1934. Corbeil did not appear on most maps before the arrival of the Quints and afterwards was listed as prominently as North Bay. *Everyone* in North America must have been fascinated with the Quints and with their every move, for each minute detail of their daily lives was recorded in all the newspapers. The little girls were raised from infancy as cloistered actresses for photographers, and personalities who could earn a lot of money for a lot of people, including themselves. No babies who were ever born had the attention the Dionnes did and no records were ever so complete and detailed as were reports of the daily development of the Quints. Publicity played a large part in all of this, because of the interest it engendered, but it was also done for medical research.

Much criticism was leveled at the handling of the Quints at the time and they were always the center of controversy. The subsequent lives of the girls were permanently affected by their upbringing and it is the gift of hindsight that shows us what went wrong. Everyone loved the Quints (and no matter how many quintuplet babies are ever born, the Dionnes will always be *The* Quints) and everyone wanted some souvenir, picture, doll or artifact of the Quints. Collectible items relating to the Quints were treasures from the beginning. The Quints were born during the worst part of the Depression of the 1930s. People wanted to look outside of their own lives and find happiness by thinking about five identical little girls who were seemingly removed from the problems of life. Money was scarce so for a small investment pleasure could be obtained from an inexpensive item that reminded an admirer of the Quints.

The birth of the Dionne Quintuplets, which was later recognized as a "miracle," was completely inauspicious and humble. At four o'clock in the morning of the 28th of May 1934, Oliva Dionne called at the home of Dr. Allan Roy Dafoe in Callander to report that his wife had entered a complicated labor two months early and that he feared for her life. Twenty-five year old Elzire had already given birth to six babies, the oldest of five surviving children being seven, and the youngest eleven months, and no other confinement had given her as much trouble as this one. There had been no prenatal care until a week prior, and no one knew what to expect.

Two local midwives had already delivered a pair of babies by the light of kerosene lamps, a third was being born when the doctor arrived and two more were aided into the world by Dr. Dafoe. The five baby girls, weighing a total of 10 pounds, 1-¼ ounces when they were first weighed at a day and a half, were wrapped in warmed blankets and placed together in a borrowed wicker basket. Dr. Dafoe did not expect the babies to live, so he hastily baptized them and sent for the priest to see the mother who also appeared to be dying. This all took place in a small frame farm house on a narrow dirt country road and the participants, all living a life of minimum existence, thought first of finances.

Oliva Dionne, married for nine years at the time of the birth of the Qunituplets, was overwhelmed by reporters. Early news accounts credit him with saying "I'm the kind of fellow they should put in jail." After this initial remark was printed in the newspapers, Oliva claimed that he was misquoted and had said, "You act like I'm the kind of fellow they should put in jail", but the original statement would not have been as interesting. His first concern was monetary, as the number of children he had to feed had doubled in a half hours' time. Newsmen said that Oliva mentioned the financial burden he had been presented with; and although he said he would do the best he could he stressed the fact that he was not exactly built for hard work, being five foot eight inches tall and weighing only one hundred and thirty pounds. Mr. and Mrs. Dionne were almost always treated unfairly by news reporters and photographers, with the exception of *The North Bay Nugget*, and were presented in such a manner as to create an unfavorable public opinion of them by selecting quotes and comments that made more exciting copy. Most quotes attributed to Mr. Dionne were ones made by the interviewer, to which he may have agreed, thus making it appear as if he had issued the statement himself.

The first quintuplet birth ever reported in Canada soon was known by the literate world. Congratulations, visitors, and the curious poured into Corbeil. With the inquiries, suggestions and telegrams arriving in the first twenty-four hours, came an invitation to exhibit the babies at the Chicago World's Fair. Oliva Dionne could not resist the offer to display his new luck and signed a contract to receive $100 per week until the Quintuplets could travel, and $250 a week once they were put on display plus all expenses and 23% of all receipts if the girls survived to go on view at the fair. 7% Was to go to Reverend Daniel Routhier, the Corbeil parish priest, who was to act as Oliva Dionne's "personal manager." These negotiations were conducted before it was known if the Quints would live.

The second day of their lives, the five tiny girls were able to take nourishment in the form of a mixture of corn syrup, milk and water administered with an eye dropper. Dr. Dafoe routinely recorded the birth of "five females" in his records when he returned to his home on the morning of May 28 and and admitted that he was surprised when he returned the next day that they were still alive. Then he began to realize what he had taken part in and quickly donated his services and needed supplies and rejected offers of assistance from other doctors. The probability of a quintuplet birth before the advent of fertility drugs was one in 57,000,000 births, and this one was the first ever in which all the babies survived. A Royal Canadian Mounted Police corporal and Red Cross Society officials accompanied a thirty-year-old hot-water incubator north from Chicago to increase the babies' chance for survival, as their birth had been **premature** and their development was about two

months below normal. Dr. Dafoe made arrangements to obtain mother's milk so the babies would gain strength, the girls were tagged to tell them apart and the mother was pronounced well enough to pose in bed with her five baby girls in a *Nugget* news photograph that was printed in every newspaper in the world. And the father wondered aloud, according to reporters, whether the cost of dressing his five daughters identically as they grew older would be a prohibitive burden for a man living on a mortgaged farm.

By May 31, Rufus C. Dawes, president of the Chicago World's Fair, said that he would not tolerate an exhibit of the Quintuplets at the exposition until their health was certain. Even Dr. Dafoe sided with the promoters in staging an exhibit. By the second of June however, at a time when two of the Quintuplets were in jeopardy of their lives, the father said that he was dissatisfied with the contract he signed to exhibit the babies at the World's Fair and that he had received an offer that he considered better. On the 59th day of their lives Attorney General Arthur W. Roebuck of Canada obtained a court order to save the Quints from "certain death in some vaudeville show" and appointed the first set of "guardians" for the new daughters of Mr. and Mrs. Oliva Dionne. Named as guardians were Dr. Allan Roy Dafoe of Callander, who was credited with keeping the infants alive longer than any other known quintuplets; W. H. Alderson of the Red Cross Emergency Committee; Kenneth Morrison, Callander merchant; and Oliver Dionne, the babies' grandfather. The guardians defied the World's Fair promoters to "take what action they please to enforce the contract," signed three days after birth, to obtain the rights to the Quints. Over vigorous parental protest, the Quints were now the responsibility of the guardians. The following March, in the custody of the guardians, they became special wards of King George V, when the Canadian government passed "An Act For The Protection Of The Dionne Quintuplets." The

Illustration 3. Elzire Dionne and the Quintuplets when they were two days old. This picture, taken by *The North Bay Nugget*, is one of the most published photographs in newspaper history. It was usually printed in "improved" versions.

Illustration 4. Postcard from Callander. Dafoe Hospital was built on the Dionne property in Corbeil.

Quints became international celebrities who were raised by professionals, their parents deemed unfit to care for them. And the Quints became millionaires.

The newspapers gave daily reports of how the babies were progressing. Charts were printed on their weight changes. Photographs were issued of the Quints being bathed, sleeping, lying, sitting, drinking from a bottle. There were pictures of Dr. Dafoe holding Yvonne, screaming in protest; nurses Louise De Kiriline and Yvonne Leroux weighing the babies; laundress Laurence Clusians with a formidable stack of clean diapers and linen; and pictures of Mama and Papa Dionne visiting their famous offspring. The Canadian Red Cross provided funds to build a special building to house the babies. The cornerstones were laid by Nurse Yvonne Leroux and Nurse Patricia Mullins; David A. Croll, Ontario Minister of Welfare, turned the key to the door as part of the dedication ceremony; and the building was named Dafoe Hospital in honor of the doctor. In late September of 1934, all the world saw pictures of the babies being carried 100 yards across the road from their birthplace to their new home. In the Nursery they would be tended by Dr. Dafoe and a staff of professionals. Their parents would be permitted to visit them if they first donned sanitary smocks and masks.

Safely inside Dafoe Hospital the Quints were properly christened by Reverend E.T.McNally, the replacement as parish priest for Father Routhier, who was relieved of his position for his part in the World's Fair scandal. The official names the girls were given were Marie Edwilda Yvonne(in honor of Nurse Leroux), Marie Lilianne Annette, Marie Emilda Cécile, Marie Jeanne Emilie and Reine Alma Marie. Mama and Papa Dionne attended the ceremony but after this time put in rare appearances at the nursery. All of this was recorded on film by Newspaper Enterprises Association, the American news service, who owned an exclusive contract for all photographs, paying $25,000 a year for this privilege, and whose photographer could enter the hospital where no other camera was ever permitted. Fred Davis was the NEA photographer who took every picture of the Quints' early years, with the exception of the first picture taken after their birth. This first picture was taken by *The North Bay Nugget*. Fred Davis later married the Quints' Nurse Leroux. The NEA contract and product endoresements furnished the funds for the Quints' nursery and its maintenance.

Dressed in bonnets, the Quints posed for their first official portraits in the new hospital nursery. Of Emilie it was said that she was the "least imperious of the five. . .demure, self-contained, last to cry at mealtime, a plain little creature with tilted nose and narrow chin." One of the nurses said, "Likely she'll be a nun." Cécile was described as "grave and circumspect" and "one could imagine her a nurse when she reaches womanhood." Annette was "peaceable, steady-nerved and calm." The nurses envisioned her as "a typical farm woman, hard-working and uncomplaining as they are in the Ontario bush, but with a spark of temper." Yvonne was to have the same destiny. They said she was "a self-assured child" and that "she expresses herself forcibly and demands her right when feeding time rolls around. She's the kind of

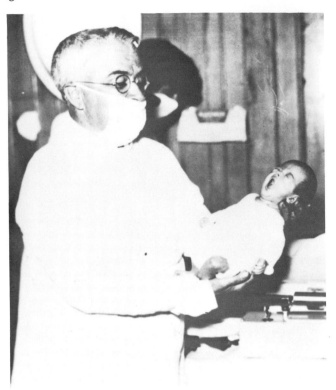

Illustration 5. Dr. Allan Roy Dafoe and Yvonne.

baby who should grow up to be a strong farm wife." Dr. Dafoe's admitted favorite was Marie. She captured the most favorable review for the papers: "Personality palm among the Dionne Quintuplets goes to Marie—prettiest, smallest, live-

liest. . .She's the type that will grow up to be an actress, say her nurses." Dr. Dafoe kept repeating that the Quints had a good chance to live and thrive as ordinary babies.

But how could they? While the babies were posing for the cameras in the community crib referred to by the nurses and attendants as "The Rat's Nest," their famous parents were in Chicago on a vaudeville tour and shopping spree. Mama admired silk pajamas presented by "smartly garbed" salesgirls and Papa visited manicure parlors looking "quite the veteran of the boulevards." They had their first champagne in "a hilarious night club," ordered their "first tailored clothes," and ate their first caviar in the Presidential Suite of the Congress Hotel. At the same time, the Premier of Ontario, Mitchell F. Hepburn, declared that the legislature would take action to "keep the babies from professional, self-seeking promoters," that he "deprecated to the fullest extent" the stage appearances of the Dionnes and that, "they have no value except as parents of the Quintuplets." They were only attempting to earn some cash.

Dr. Dafoe fared better on his first tour. In 1935 he went to New York City where Alfred E. Smith, former New York Governor and Herbert Hoover's opponent for the Presidency in 1928, escorted him to the top of the Empire State Building. He met with noted physicians and obstetricians and he dined with the mother of President Roosevelt. In Washington, D.C. he was a guest of the Canadian Embassy. Everywhere he was praised for saving the lives of the Quints. The Academy

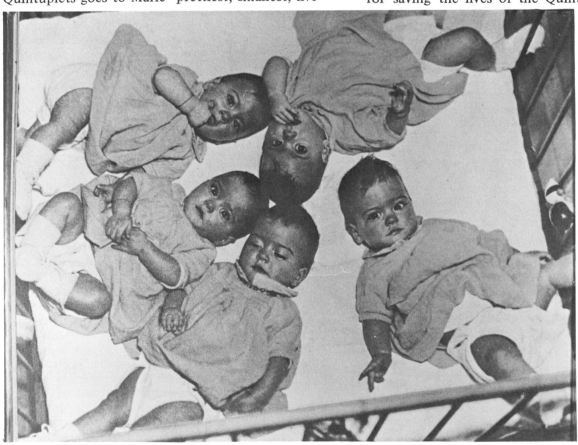

Illustration 6. The Quints before their first birthday in the communal crib called the "Rat's Nest" by the staff of Dafoe Hospital. Clockwise from upper left: Marie, Emilie, Annette, Yvonne and Cécile.

of Medicine in Toronto had already presented him
with a document recognizing his "high scientific
attainments." He admitted that he kept the babies
alive in the early days with a "half a drop, maybe
a drop" of rum. In New York while he was sightseeing, he was given a copy of a respected scientific
work on obstetrics. After glancing at it he remark-
ed that it was "too deep" for him. Yet he was only
criticized by Mama and Papa Dionne, who wanted
control of their own children.

Even Mrs. Benoit LaBelle and Mrs. Donalda
Legros, the midwives who assisted in the birth of
the Quints, told their stories to the papers—and
set up their own stands to sell souvenirs and display memorabilia from their work.

In *"We Were Five,"* the biography of the
Dionne Quintuplets, written by James Brough with
Annette, Cécile, Marie and Yvonne Dionne, the
Quints state:

> "The happiest, least complicated years of our lives
> were spent in the nursery...We had everything we wanted,
> everything within the limits of our knowledge and imagina-
> tions. In that house of fives, we were like princesses."
> (pgs. 53-54)

In the Nursery, every aspect of their lives was
photographed and recorded. Almost daily pictures
of the Quints appeared in American newspapers.
Specal full-page reports were issued for birthdays
and for every Canadian and American holiday. Of
course these events were staged well in advance so
that the pictures could be distributed in plenty of
time for NEA customers. The babies smelled Easter
lilies and eyed chocolate rabbits; they peered up
over their birthday cakes with wide-open, shining
eyes and toasted themselves with milk; they smiled
from behind the frames of cardboard valentines;
they looked out of Christmas wreaths, quizzically
studied Christmas trees and pulled the fake beard
of Dr. Dafoe dressed as Santa—and the following
day they displayed their presents on Page One. For
holidays that are not celebrated in Canada they
were equally cooperative. On Thanksgiving they
offered thanks for the blessings they had received
and prayed for the unfortunate. Once they were
beyond the age of posing coyly in a "Thanksgiving Basket" they were shown munching drum-
sticks, smelling freshly cooked turkeys or chasing a
live one—and later breaking its wishbone. On the
Fourth of July they were seen on the front page
lounging in a hammock, having found a "safe and
sane way to spend it." On Labor Day they were depicted at play, "not violating the rule of no work."

In 1938 the NEA photographer posed the
Quints in a series of nursery rhyme stories, complete with elaborate costumes, the needed props,
stage setting, scripts and credits. The series included such favorites as "Old King Cole" (with Yvonne
as the King, Marie as a page and the other girls as
fiddlers); "Mary, Mary, Quite Contrary" (with
Yvonne in the lead role again); "Hickory Dickory
Dock" (with fake mouse and clock); and the greatest production of all: "Cinderella" (Yvonne once
more captured the lead role.) This last picture pre-

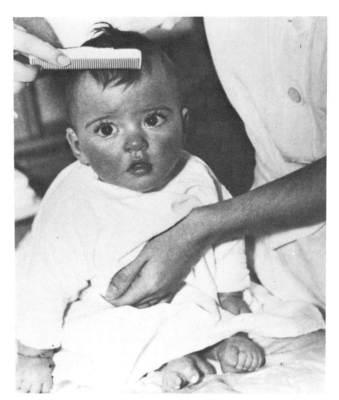
Illustration 7. Cécile. April 1935.

sentation ran for five days at the end of 1938 and
included seventeen scenes.

The Quints became full-blown actresses for
Twentieth Century-Fox Studios when they were
signed by Darryl F. Zanuck to appear in fictionalized movie versions of their lives. They were already "pros" as their first international public per-
formance went back to their first birthday when
they cooed and chortled into Canadian Broadcasting Corporation microphones for live audiences all
over North America. Their films were *The Country
Doctor* and *Reunion* in 1936 and *Five of a Kind* in

Illustration 8. Thanksgiving 1935.

Illustration 9. Second Birthday, 1936. Left to right: Cécile, Marie, Yvonne, Emilie and Annette.

1938. For their services, the "stars" account was credited with $50,000 before filming began. After *The Country Doctor* proved to be a financial success, the studio produced another check for $250,000, which included payment for three more films, although only two were completed. Mr. Zanuck, whose most valuable studio asset at the time was little Shirley Temple, had originally planned to release a Dionne feature film every year on an indefinite schedule.

During their childhood, weekly news features by Pathe were shown in theaters across the country. These films ran from about five to fifteen minutes and similar reels could be purchased for home viewing. The still pictures from all the films were owned by NEA.

Summers were especially busy and lucrative seasons for the little actresses. Thousands of Americans and Canadians made the goal of their summer vacation a drive to northern Ontario over dirt roads to see the Quintuplets in person. In the first year of the Quints' birth, a specially paved road had been constructed from Callander to the Quints' home by the government so that Dr. Dafoe would waste no time in case of an emergency. This two-mile stretch of road was one of the best highways in North America before World War II, and the only paved road in the region. It was also an opportune convenience for visitors driving out to see the Quints. It was estimated that an average weekday brought 3,000 visitors, and that on weekends and holidays there were about 8,000. Of the 100,000 visitors who arrived each summer in the early years, an estimated 70,000 were from the

Illustration 10. Left. Annette 1937.

Illustration 11. Below. Marie, Dr. Dafoe's favorite, in his hat. January 1937.

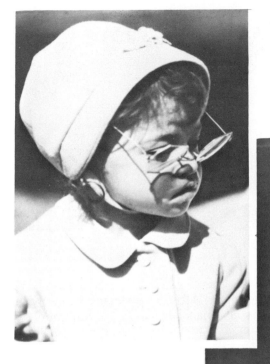

Illustration 12. Right. Emilie, wearing the glasses of one of her nurses. October 1936.

Illustration 13. Far right. Yvonne.

United States. Many visitors stayed in the vicinity and returned each day to see the Quints. There were morning and afternoon "visits."

The Dionne Quintuplets were one of the Depressions's leading industries. *Harpers* magazine reported in November of 1938 that the annual value of the American tourist traffic to Ontario was estimated at between $1,000,000 and $125,000,000. The report stated that in an average year the potential earning power of the Quints and Quint-inspired industries could be nearly a billion dollars, which would leave them with few industrial rivals in the world.

The curious who came to see the Quints walked past a hollow building surrounding an open-air playground, with concrete walk, grass, a sand pile, a wading pool and an assortment of toys. The runway through which visitors passed was soundproofed and was separated from the playing Quints by a wire-mesh fence and heavy one-way glass. This was so that the visitors could stare at the Quints without their knowing it. (They claim in their autobiography that they were always aware of what was going on and that they enjoyed it.) In rainy weather when there were less visitors, the Quints appeared on the porch of the nursery and half-heartedly sang simple French-Canadian folk songs such as "Frère Jacques."

Outside of the building, memento savers could purchase stones from Dionne property, postcards, food and calendars personally autographed by Oliva Dionne himself, who cleared about $16,000 a season from his own souvenir pavilion.

At the time of the Quintuplets' birth, Callander was an abandoned lumber town. Four years later it was a prosperous community where nearly everyone had a job. There were sleeping accommodations for 1,500 visitors and the outlying roads were lined with tourist cabins. By 1938, from visitors alone, the gross take deposited in the Quints' account amounted to $750,000. Additional thousands were earned from product endorsements.

Dr. Dafoe praised the conduct of visitors for the newspapers, and in 1936 proudly cited that thirty honeymoon couples had visited his home in Callander. He criticized those who claimed that his wards were making a fortune and pointed out that it cost $18,000 a year to maintain the nursery.

In 1937 the University of Toronto's School for Child Study published their findings, *A Biological Study of the Dionne Quintuplets, An Identical Set.* For this study the doctors and nurses had carefully charted every nuance of the childrens' development. From their studies the specialists concluded that the Dionne Quintuplets had originated from one fertilized egg. One split in the egg produced Yvonne and Annette, the other produced Cécile and another ovum that twinned to give Emilie and Marie. The last split resulted in a mirror pair of twins. Emilie was left-handed and her hair whorl was clockwise. The others were all right-handed with the hair whorl counterclockwise. They all belonged to blood group O; all their eyes were medium brown, flecked with gray; between all their second and third toes they had "a mild

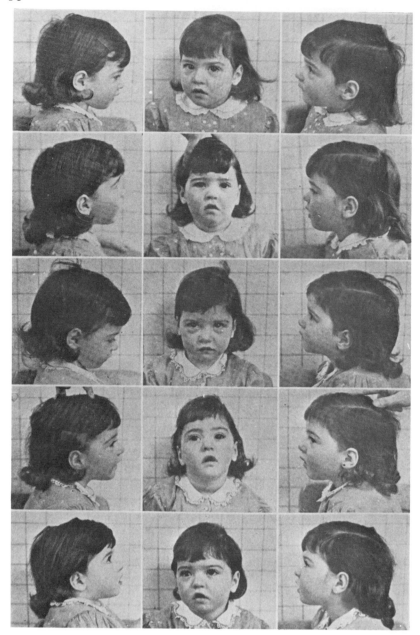

Illustration 14. Full-face views and left and right profiles from the University of Toronto's medical studies, 1937. The Quints are, from top to bottom: Emilie, Yvonne, Cécile, Marie and Annette.

ing, bladder control and bowel elimination.

When Annette, the first Quint to cut a tooth, was found to do so, it was front page news in March of 1935. As the "scientists" reported, the Quints were slow to develop language ability. On October 22, 1935, the front pages of the papers reported that "to Emilie Dionne goes the honor of being the first Quintuplet to say a word." The first spoken word was supposed to have been "Mama," and Mrs. Elzire Dionne was supposed to have been present in the nursery when it was uttered. At this time, Yvonne had been walking alone for several weeks; Emilie had already taken her first steps a few days previously; and the others could take some steps with a nurse's help.

Less attention was given to litigation brought by the parents of the Quints to have full charge of their children and full charge of their bank accounts. The Dionne parents brought an action against the government and against the guardians soon after they were appointed. They had appealed their case to King George V of England and his wife, imploring the Queen as a mother; and they had written a letter of protest to Pope Pius XI. Reunion was eventually obtained by more subtle means.

In the Nursery the Quints were first-class stars. Every picture ot them shows careful coaching and stage direction. They looked up eagerly from five identical "low chairs." They all posed willingly in the same bathtub. They played joyously with any number of toys, dolls and stuffed animals. They enthusiastically modeled their newest fashions. Annette banged on a drum, Yvonne blew on a trumpet, Marie pounded a tiny piano, Emilie puffed on a saxophone and Cécile chewed the keys of another trumpet—all facing Fred Davis' camera. The nurses were on the sidelines and Dr. Dafoe, by now a veteran showman, was in the center, letting them try on his big boots or guiding a childish hand as it composed a letter to Santa Claus. They had a good time in their Easter finery or bundled up in heavy snowsuits, and the papers reported that "clothes made the girl." It was even news when the "nursery became silent with the afternoon sandman in charge."

They were full-time performers. And it was their own lives that were the scripts. No one can deny that they were very cute and very appealing.

form of syndactlus," a thin membrane of skin; their hair and the color of skin was identical. The palm prints and the sole prints of the Quintuplets further proved that they had originated from a single egg as they were so uniform.

The Nursery was an ideal place to scientifically observe a matched set of quintuplets. Medical records accounted for only twenty-seven authentic cases of quintuplets before the birth of the Dionnes, although many others were reported. The evidence tabulated tells that mothers of quintuplets (before fertility drugs) usually had given birth to several babies previously. Dr. Dafoe also reported that during the third month of her pregnancy Mrs. Dionne had labor-like pains and passed an aborted embryo, although the twinning process does produce odd or even numbers naturally. Careful charts were maintained to show the Quints' development in play, dresssing habits, sleeping, eat-

It made the headlines when one had a cold. It was news when they donned sunglasses. They always looked happy and the doctor continued to pronounce them "normal." Their daily routines, their diets and the weight and measurement charts were printed regularly throughout their nursery years. And every birthday was happier than the last. As the Depression progressed and the world political condition worsened, the admiring public clamored for more of this vicarious happiness.

The Dionne Quintuplets gave babies the best publicity they ever had. Newspapers promoted "Baby Week" and ran special features on babies, again showing the latest poses of the most famous babies in the world. The first birthday of the Quints was named "Adopt a Child Week" by Canada's Welfare Minister, David Croll. Applications to adopt children poured in from all over Canada and "shelters" and children's homes were "going out of business." The welfare workers noticed a distinct preference for girls in the applications, and in some communities the proportion was as high as nine out of ten. Minister Croll hoped that "the Dionne babies' first birthday may be turned into a blessing for hundreds of children everywhere."

Contests were held throughout the United States and Canada for Quint look-alikes. In the summer of 1937 the winner of the prize in Toledo, Ohio, was Master James Joseph Leonard, three, attired in garb like the Quints' own and with his hair in the same curls. His mother revealed the hoax after the contest was over and James had won the prize as the baby who most resembled the famous Canadian sisters.

Babies and children could be shown pictures of the Quints vigorously and enthusiastically brushing their teeth, and willingly submitting to dental examinations by Dr. Dafoe and the dentists brought in from Toronto. Mothers were informed that the Quints received anti-diptheria toxoids and innoculations against smallpox and that every precaution was taken to secure them from colds. Many a doctor was given the responsibility of keeping children as healthy as Dr. Dafoe did the Dionnes.

The Quints were shown grinning and laughing, in "high good humor," and were reported to be "jolly" before they underwent an operation for the removal of their tonsils and adenoids in November of 1938. Constant physical checkups were always stressed to maintain good health.

Magazines during the 1930s did a brisk business because of the Quints. Cover portraits and specially commissioned paintings helped to guarantee sales and renew subscriptions.

Writers for the magazines wondered about the fate of the other five Dionne children. It was reported that the older children were not envious or jealous. They soon formed their own opinions, however, for they developed inferiority complexes over resentment of their more famous siblings. In some articles the parents were said to be "simple

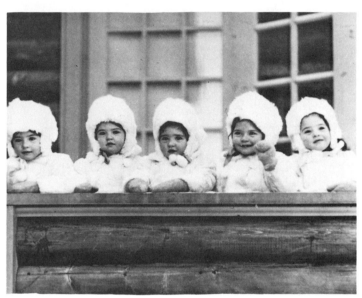

Illustration 15. Summer 1937. From left to right: Annette, Emilie, Cécile, Marie and Yvonne.

Illustration 16. From left to right: Emilie, Annette, Yvonne, Cécile and Marie on the porch of Dafoe Hospital. February 1938.

and unassuming." Others accused them of having acquired a taste for luxurious living. In 1935 Papa Dionne scorned a showman's offer to replace his house and pay him $10,000 a year to exhibit the Quints' birthplace. Yet he did prefer to drive Cadillacs.

Dr. Dafoe became an advisory editor for *Parents' Magazine* and Clara Savage Littledale, the editor, journeyed north to Corbeil to personally appraise the situation and inform curious readers that the Quints were indeed "pretty, sturdy and bright." She found that the sisters were "more cunning and bubbling over with spirits and health than their pictures could possibly show." Parents

Illustration 17. Christmas 1937.

Illustration 18. Christmas 1937. From left to right: Annette, Yvonne, Cécile, Emilie and Marie.

all over the continent were instructed that the "modern emphasis on right feeding, rest, habit training and careful routine" had resulted in "five of the plumpest, merriest, prettiest little sisters you can imagine."

Time admitted in May of 1937 that the Quints owed their success to the "sturdy stock" of their parents and their ancestors. *Better Homes and*

Illustration 19. Left to right: Yvonne, Emilie, Marie, Cécile and Annette. 1939.

Gardens in September of 1937 said that Dr. Dafoe was raising the Quints to be "throughly healthy, normal, brave and joyous..."and that they would be able to "face all the trials and problems of a difficult world without batting an eye." Their destiny was to be far different, and it was partly Dafoe's fault.

Speculation on the development of the Dionne Quintuplets provided forums and seminars for psychologists from all over the United States and Canada. They all agreed on one thing: the Quints' birth had changed many lives. All the writers, child psychologists, dietitians and infant studiers wondered in print about the future of the girls. Most conceded that they were being reared properly and that parents everywhere should emulate the examples of their training. Few worried much over the long-range effect on the Quints of their being the center of a battle between their parents and Canadian officials.

Papa Dionne was providing news copy in early 1936 by applying to King Edward VIII to have the custody of the famous Quints restored to their parents. According to the father, Mama Dionne was "sad" and even a shopping trip to New York City did not lift her spirits. A mother's heart had been broken by a heartless government. Papa Dionne justifiably pointed out that a free government had no right to deny parents the custody of their own children.

Dr. Dafoe found himself the defendant in a libel suit in the spring of 1939 when Mr. Dionne claimed that the doctor held the family up to ridicule by being initiated into the Circus Saints and Sinners Club in New York City, in which Dafoe wore a gown marked "Doctor of Litters" and carried a bag inscribed "Mass Deliveries." The doctor's conduct certainly invited criticism.

In February of 1939 Oliva Dionne told *True Story* magazine that the famous babies were strangers to their own parents. In the report he stated,

> "I have often lain awake at night, and wondered if the millions who have looked so delightedly at the pictures of the babies, if the thousands who have traveled to Corbeil to watch them at play, realized what a frightful ordeal we, their parents, were enduring."

Oliva's ghostwriter goes on to plead his case. He tells that his family were "hard-working and enterprising pioneers." He cites how much Elzire cried at the loss of her babies until her "eyes had been wrung dry."

The account neglects to mention the plan that Oliva and Elzire had devised and which ultimately worked. The Catholic Church was enlisted for support and French-speaking Canadians were drawn into the conflict because it could be pointed out that the Quints were being denied their rightful heritage living in the Nursery, although they had always been instructed in the Catholic religion and by court order were learning to speak French rather than English. (Mrs. Dionne only spoke French; Mr. Dionne was more fluent in English than in French.) The other Dionne children told news reporters that they cried to see the Quints in "jail" (the Nursery).

What child has control of its own destiny? Babies are at the complete mercy of those who care for them. When the Quints were old enough to understand, Mama gained their support in the fight. Bribes of candy (not doled out so generously in Dafoe Hospital) caused the Quints to say special prayers and to tell visiting priests about them; and for the benefit of reporters, to publicly beg to be reunited with their parents. What child would not?

In the same issue of *True Story* in which Papa Dionne pleaded his case the rebuttal, "A Distinguished Canadian Replies to Papa Dionne" by Thomas Wayling, "noted Ottawa Newspaper Correspondent," gave the other side of the story:

The guardians did not keep the children away from their parents, and although they only lived one hundred yards away, they seldom visited them. When the Quints were two days old, Papa Dionne and the parish priest concluded the infamous contract to exhibit the babies in Chicago, lessening their chances of survival. The American vaudeville tour further pointed out the parents' intents. The Dionnes were paid $100 per month for their expenses by the guardians, and the other Dionne children were being educated in private schools by the guardians at the cost of $6,000 a year, and without the attention of Dr. Dafoe the Quints would never have lived.

Both sides presented valid arguments. But because they could only reason within the limits of their own experience, the parents had prejudiced their position from the beginning. Newspaper sensationalism did the rest.

The Quints themselves were the subject for the front pages in the spring of 1939. In March, newspapers carried the headlines " 'Royal Snubbing' Riles Ontario" and "Action of King and Queen Arouses Indignation in Canada." It was learned that when the King and Queen of England visited Canada in the summer of 1939 their itinerary did not include a scheduled stop to visit the Quints, although they would pass within eighty miles of their home. The Mayor of North Bay, Arthur Beattie, on behalf of the people of Northern Ontario, who were hurt and humiliated by the "snub" said, "I think I speak for most people—and it's a great disappointment to me." Judge H. A. Valin, one of the guardians at the time, expressed his view: "Every important person who has ever visited this area has come to see the children. I can't believe that their Majesties won't find some time to see the babies."

The problem was solved when it was decided that the Quints would travel to Toronto in a special railway car to be received by the King and Queen. On may 22, 1939, the *Erie* (Pennsylvania) *Daily Times* carried the headline: "Dionne Quintuplets Salute, Kiss Queen Elizabeth." A lower-placed headline was "Hitler, Duce Sign Ten-Year War Pact." On the same day, the *Cleveland News* carried their headline in two lines of large print: "Dr. Dafoe Tells of Quints' Antics As They Charmed King and Queen." The secondary headline was "Quints Kiss the Queen But Yvonne Saves a Handshake For King." The Quints' traveling outfits and

Illustration 20. May 1939. The Quints arrive in Toronto to meet the King and Queen. The Quints, left to right: Emilie, Cécile, Yvonne, Marie and Annette. The escorts, left to right: Nurse O'Shaughnessy; Gaetane Vezina, the Quint's teacher; and Nurse Corriveau.

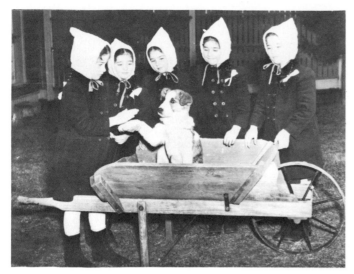

Illustration 21. Top left. Six years old.

Illustration 22. Bottom left. The Quints at six with two of their brothers.

Illustration 23. Top right. One of Dr. Dafoe's last visits with the Quints, early 1942. The girls are, left to right: Emilie, Marie, Annette, Cécile and Yvonne. Nurse Beatrice Provenchero is on the right.

the gowns in which they were received by the royal couple were depicted on the front pages.

The visit to Toronto also closed a long chapter in the Quints' lives. Newspaper Enterprise Association Service, Inc. had furnished the world with thousands of photographs of the Dionne Quintuplets over the years. The contract with NEA expressly stated that the guardians were to protect the girls from all other cameras. But as the train carrying the Dionnes and Dr. Dafoe pulled into Toronto, news photographers were on hand. The girls could not resist a peek out of the train window and for the first time they walked out in public view, "unprotected" from other cameras. The prying lens of outside news services managed to sneak in several snaps of the youngsters. The guardians failed to shield their charges and the contract was breached. Never again would pictures of the Quints be taken on such a regular schedule.

Mama Dionne, at the time of the visit to Toronto, stated that the Queen was "very royal, but very nice." She was also offended that the King and Queen did not express a wish to be presented with the other Dionne children. The Quints returned to Corbeil with blue reefer coats, gifts from the Princesses Elizabeth and Margaret Rose.

Almost everyone who visited the Quints in their nursery agreed on one thing: They were the sweetest, most innocent little girls imaginable. They could not help having been spoiled, being the center of adult attention all their lives, and participating in the battle between parents and professional guardians. All the doctors and psychologists who investigated them found them to be entirely "normal" children. By the time they were six, the girls were big for their age. Their average height was 45½ inches and their average weight was 51 pounds. They were cheerfully extroverted, alert and full of natural curiosity. The only area in which they were backward was in speech. Most products of multiple birth, or children of relatively the same ages who are raised together, develop their own system of communication and a private vocabulary. In general, the Quints spoke with a limited vocabulary of French-Canadian patois. They were always intensely loyal to one another.

In 1939 the adults who managed the Quints were making plans that would permanently affect their lives. In January the guardians rejected an offer for $500,000 with a written guarantee of $100,000, for a personal appearance at the New York World's Fair that year. Papa Dionne was now one of the guardians. He had learned his lesson but he still planned to exploit available opportunities, for by July he brought litigation to have all contracts using the names of the Dionne Quintuplets turned over to him. Most of these contracts had been signed by Dr. Dafoe. These and other legal actions taken against Dr. Dafoe by the Dionne parents were settled by the later part of 1939 with an agreement in which the parents would receive the advertising accounts and would drop the libel suit against Dafoe that resulted from his appearance before the Saints and Sinners Club in New York City. Then Dr. Dafoe officially resigned his post as guardian of the Quintuplets, although he was to remain as their physician. At the time Dr. Dafoe and the other guardians claimed that they favored a plan to have the entire Dionne family all living under the same roof. As part of the legal settlement, a common dwelling house was to be erected for the entire Dionne family.

This new house was called "the saddest home we ever knew" by the Quints (page 100, *We Were Five*). It was a nineteen-room, nine-bathroom mansion built entirely from Quintuplet funds at the cost of $75,000. The furnishings cost about $12,000. At the time, it was one of the largest homes ever built in northern Canada and the most elaborate Corbeil ever had. This house was a sharp contrast to the small frame home without plumbing that it overlooked—the frame farm house in which the Quints were born. Shortly after the Quints moved into the "Big House" they posed for their tenth birthday pictures for national magazines.

Their value as attractions would not be lost, as the Quints were still not free to run about in public. The news pictures were staged to help prove to the public that the Quints loved their family. They posed with their mother instructing them in sewing; playing with their brothers and sisters; receiving school instruction with them in the former nursery, which was now officially a government approved classroom; they grouped around Papa in his private study; and all the Dionnes ate together at the same dining room table. The Quints were instructed to kiss their parents dutifully and to love them and to be compatible with the other Dionne children. But years of resentment over the control of the girls had formed strong attitudes.

The girls were spoiled "princesses" when they came to live in the Big House. Their renown had brought fame and prosperity to themselves, to their family, to all those who managed them and to the country around Corbeil and Callander. Between the Dionne parents and Dr. Dafoe, who represented those who denied them their Quints, there was a clash of personalities, of religions, of languages and of money aims. Elzire, a woman whose only goal in life was to be a good wife and mother, was now quick-tempered and suspicious. Oliva, the

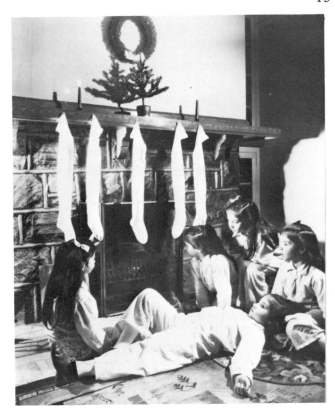

Illustration 24. Top photo. Christmas in Dafoe Hospital. 1942.

Illustration 25. Middle photo. In May of 1943 the Quints and their mother traveled to Superior, Wisconsin, to christen five cargo ships as their part in the War effort.

Illustration 26. Bottom photo. The "Big House," the Dionne Mansion in the early 1940's.

Illustration 27. The Quints looking at the house where they were born from a front window of the Big House. Early 1944.

Illustration 29. All of the Dionnes together. Clockwise, beginning with Papa Dionne, at the head of the table: Mama, Oliva Jr., Pauline, Marie, Rose Marie, Yvonne, Ernest, Victor, Cécile, Daniel, Emilie, Therese and Annette. 1944.

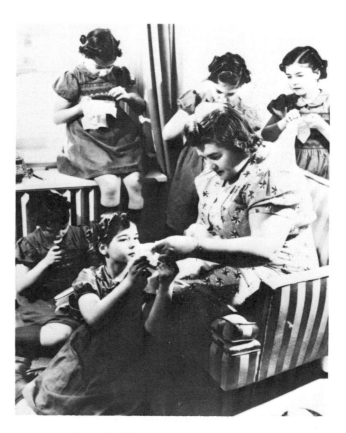

Illustration 30. Sewing lessons with Mama.

Illustration 28. With Papa in his private study before their 10th Birthday.

father, was under forty, but was deeply cynical after the seven-year fight for the custody of his own children.

The Quints had personally witnessed outbursts of anger and physical violence, such as the time their parents staged an unsuccessful "sit-in" at Dafoe Hospital. The doctor told them one thing and their parent told them another. The Quints' personalities suffered as a result of adult personality conflicts and their living situations. The scene was pitiful in the early years when the Quints came into the world in the simple frame farm house and Oliva could not have managed without outside help. While Elzire was still in bed, recovering from the birth of five children at one time, a screen was put between her and the babies by the nurses hired by Dr. Dafoe to keep them isolated from "outside contact." Yet reporters and photographers could peer at them under the nurses' supervision.

Before the arrival of the Quints the Dionnes had never encountered any experience with promoters and money seekers whose chief goals were financial. Oliva's concern was also financial so he let himself accept improper advice. Dr. Dafoe was not adverse to exhibiting the Quints at first, but once his appointment as guardian was official he insisted on complete control. His devotion was complete, though.

The task of Dafoe and the nurses was to save the lives of the babies and perhaps they were overzealous in their duty. The parents could only visit their children under hospital rules—which lasted for years. They could rarely hold the girls and the other children were not permitted near them. Mrs. Dionne was a mother first and her every instinct was to feed and clothe her own babies. The nurses and the doctor prevented all this, never explaining to Elzire that they were trying to help her. Dr. Dafoe was not diplomatic with the parents; and guards prevented them from passing locked gates and doors, behind which lived half of their family. During the years that the Quints were in the Nursery, they only had one or two nurses at a time. But all told there were fourteen different nurses, which in itself speaks for the conditions under which everything operated.

The press and the Hollywood films made the parents out to be ignorant peasants of the backwoods variety, when in reality they were no less financially or educationally deprived than their neighbors and in most instances, probably better off. Dafoe gained all the prominence and the favorable publicity. 1934 Was a time by which medical science was able to make more likely the survival of quintuplets(as compared to 1904, when it was not, i.e.) and Dr. Dafoe could not have done more than another devoted doctor.

Dr. Dafoe was an unsophisticated country doctor in a simple farm community before the Quints were born. Afterwards, he assumed many of the philosophical and folksy ways portrayed by Jean Hersholt in the film versions of the Quints' lives. The newsmen were his friends for he gave

Illustration 31. Posing with their Shirley Temple dolls in the 27 by 15-foot living room of the Big House before their 10th birthday in 1944. Left to right: Marie, Annette, Yvonne, Cécile and Emilie.

them the Quints. Oliva Dionne could only give newsmen his frustration and his mistrust. He had been misrepresented too many times and he no longer believed in justice or fairness.

After 1941 the Quints insisted on speaking only in French. This was because their parents asked them to, having at least one difference over Dafoe. In early 1941, Dr. Dafoe had been away for two months to undergo a serious operation. When he returned to the Nursery he noticed a change in the girls. His influence over them, once so powerful, had fallen under the determined pressure and continued opposition of Mama and Papa Dionne. They no longer loved and trusted the doctor so he resigned his position as their personal physician. The day Dr. Dafoe resigned, the metal plaque bearing his name was removed from the stone gates in front of Dafoe Hospital. Later the Quints were reunited with a family that they hardly knew and they discovered that it was not an entrance to happiness. Eight-year-old girls do not know what adults have in mind for them.

The Quints in their autobiography said they were relegated to the basement of the mansion. (It is above ground level.) Furthermore the Quints stated that they were served less appetizing meals than the rest of the Dionne family. They felt like the "servants" for the other members of the household because each had an assigned schedule of chores and work details to perform. They would be pampered and spoiled no more. But it was in the Big House that the girls learned that things are not as they seem. They were told how their birth had adversely affected a once happy family; how public control of their lives had ruined their mother's health because of grief; and how the birth of babies in itself was an unpleasant and exhausting trial that should be avoided. Yet they saw that Mrs. Dionne had given birth to three more babies after they were born.

Illustration 32. The Quints being shown a soundphoto machine by Charles J. Nichols of International News Photos. Left to right: Emilie, Marie, Nichols, Yvonne, Cécile and Annette. February 1946.

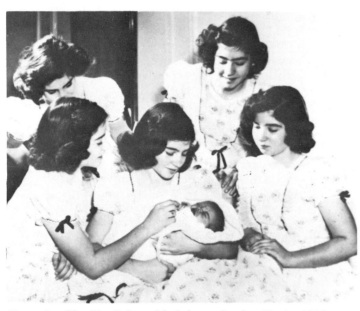

Illustration 33. The Quints with their new brother Claude. 1946.

The years prior to and during puberty are critical ones in personality formation and in adjustment to adult life. The impressions and opinions formed during this time permanently affect attitudes and adjustments to adult responsibilities. In gerneral, during these important formative years, the Quints were made to feel inferior and they were constantly reminded that they were not "miracles" but were an awkward and unwelcome accident. Time after time, over the years, the Quints were told, "We were better off before you were born, and we'd be better off without you now" (page 112, *We Were Five*).

The Dionne parents would not have consciously set out to alter the personalities of the Quints. Their reactions were based on emotion and they were bitter and disappointed by how life had treated them. Outsiders had denied them the right to their own destiny and the control of their own children. It was deemed that the parents would not have acted wisely in the rearing of the girls, and that money considerations would receive first priority; but the parents, who were thrust into international attention overnight, did not have a chance to prove what they could have done with the proper advice. Mama and Papa were not deliberately vengeful, but they saw their Quintuplets as the root of all their personal problems. The parents did not realize that childhood experiences form adult attitudes, impressions, opinions and reactions.

On February 14, 1942, Dr.Allan Roy Dafoe officially resigned his position as personal physician of the Dionne Quintuplets. His only statement was, "I feel my period of usefulness is over." The Quints had made Dr. Dafoe as famous as they were themselves. In countless interviews and personally scripted articles, Dafoe reiterated over the years his part in assuring the survival of the girls from their first precarious days of birth. He had refused lucrative offers to head clinics and had remained in Callander, close to the Quints, from the time the Dafoe Hospital opened in 1934. Yet the doctor was not adverse to basking in publicity and was included in advertising data, for which he was accused of personal gain.

Dr. Dafoe was a descendant of ordinary Canadian farm folk. Following his mother's wishes, he attended college and medical school and became a "country doctor," tending the people of the Callander area until, at age fifty-one, he assisted in the delivery of the Dionne Quintuplets. Gradually Dafoe gave up his practice, devoting his time and energy to the Quints. He visited them every morning in the nursery and spent his afternoons receiving visitors and writers and in answering his correspondence with the aid of a secretary. The Quints became his life. Reportedly, he was never paid for his work in delivering the babies. His bill came to $153.31.

In June of 1943, a year after he had resigned his post as the Quints' doctor, Dafoe died of pneumonia. He had lost his reason for living. He had given all he had to the Quints, and when he lost them, he lost everything. The last farewell had been shortly after the resignation and the Quints admit that they received him icily, wanting to please their parents at his expense. Although Dafoe utilized the advantages he had been presented with because of the Quints, they never again had another friend who would protect them from personal exploitation.

In the Big House the Dionne Quintuplets were not the center of Continental attention as they had been as babies. They were no longer photographed daily and the public did not see their continuing development on such a regular basis in the newspapers. Every birthday was still a news event and it was reported and pictured as before, but not with the same enthusiasm.

Illustration 34. Top left. April 1947. The bridesmaid dresses the Quints wore when their brother Ernest married Jeannette Guindon. The newlyweds set up housekeeping in the former "Staff House." *International News Photo.*

Illustration 35. Top right. Mama Dionne on her way to Europe, July 1949. *International News Photo.*

Illustration 36. The Quints assist in the wedding of sister Rose Marie in the summer of 1949. Left to right: Emilie, Cécile, Maurice and Rose Marie Girouard, Annette, Marie and Yvonne. *International News Photo.*

One reason for this diminishing enthusiasm was that the Quints were no longer as "cute." As young ladies they were criticized for not being attractive. (Everyone's looks were measured by Hollywood standards in those days.) They were at sixteen, five feet, two inches (except for Marie who was two inches shorter) and inclined to be plump. They were terribly shy and were not the accomplished "performers" they had once been. An analysis shows that, not withstanding the unattractive styles in women's clothing and the hairdos of the late forties and early fifties, they had no concept of how to dress to a flattering advantage. They did not wear their hair in a becoming style or use makeup that would make them look prettier. They dressed according to the tastes of their mother, and wore outfits that would be more appropriate for her, making them seem matronly and old for their age. Their personal expression had been arrested once they were under exclusive parental care.

In their own right they were wealthy, but they never had any fun with their money. Boyfriends were completely out of the question.

The former Dafoe Hospital, the nursery where the girls recorded their happiest memories of childhood, was turned into a private school known as Villa Notre Dame. Three nuns from the Sisters of the Assumption instructed the Quints and ten other French-Canadian girls, selected by the Sisters so that the Quints would become used to "outsiders." The Villa Notre Dame cost $72,000 a year and all expenses were paid by Quintuplet funds. "School" consisted of a very regimented schedule. The girls rose at six-thirty every morning and attended Mass in their own private chapel with their own priest. They then "helped" their mother with the breakfast, cleared the dishes and straightened up the house before they were in class by eight-thirty. (The other Dionne children were in private boarding schools again.) From noon to one-thirty they ate dinner and were involved with the chores pertaining to it. Then it was back to class until six, the last two hours having been set aside for homework. At six was supper, more chores and they were in bed by nine-thirty. The parents claimed that they were unable to secure outside "help."

As visiting celebrities, the Dionne Quintuplets and the other girls of Villa Notre Dame were

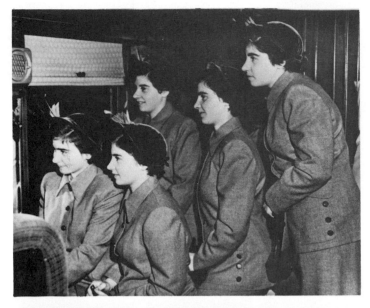

Illustration 37. Top left. Arriving in New York City by train, October 1950. Seated, left to right: Yvonne and Annette. Standing, left to right: Cécile, Marie and Emilie. *International News Photo.*

Illustration 38. Bottom left. At the Waldorf-Astoria Hotel in New York City, October 1950. Left to right: Francis Cardinal Spellman, Yvonne, Marie, Emilie, Oliva Dionne, Governor Thomas E. Dewey, Vice-President Alben W. Barkley, Cécile and Annette. *International News Photo.*

Illustration 39. Top right. In New York for the Alfred E. Smith Memorial Dinner, at which they sang, October 1950. Left to right: Emilie, Marie, Annette, Yvonne and Cécile.

escorted to New York City for the first time by Oliva Dionne in October of 1950. The Quints were hosted by Francis Cardinal Spellman and every move they made was recorded by the cameras of various news services. The highlight of the stay was a banquet, the sixth annual dinner of the Alfred E. Smith Memorial Foundation, a charity honoring the former Catholic presidential candidate, at which the girls would sing French-Canadian folk songs. The Cardinal met the Quints at their train in Grand Central Station where they were mobbed by the curious.

In preparation for the banquet at the Waldorf-Astoria Hotel, the Quints were taken to a beauty shop where they were treated to five equally un-attractive and identical hairdos. Wearing formless floor-length gowns, capes and their "first high heels," the girls were received at the one-hundred-dollar-a-plate dinner by Vice-President Alben W. Barkley, Governor Thomas E. Dewey, former New York City Mayor and Ambassador to Mexico William O'Dwyer and Acting Mayor Impellitteri.

Monseigneur Gustav Schultheiss, Cardinal Spellman's representative, escorted the Quints around New York on a sightseeing trip, taking in such attractions as the Statue of Liberty, the view from the top of the RCA Building and St. Patrick's Cathedral. At Alfred E. Smith Memorial Hospital they admired newborn infants. They also journeyed to Brooklyn to present gifts to the quadruplet children of Mr. and Mrs. Charles Collins. Movie star Margaret O'Brien, who was their same age, paid them a surprise visit at the convent where they were staying. At the end of the four-day visit, the Quints, speaking through Cardinal Spellman, said that they "enjoyed everything" and that they had a "wonderful time."

As they had always done, the Quints posed obligingly throughout their stay, wearing bulky coats, uncomplimentary gowns that were too large in size for them and hats usually worn by older women.

In June of 1952, shortly after their eighteenth birthday, the Quints graduated from high school at the Villa Notre Dame. Legally, in Ontario they were free to marry now without parental consent, as was stated in all reports of the event. They had not, as yet, been alone with a boy other than their little brother Claude, who was five at the time.

The Quintuplets were raised to maintain a strict belief in the Catholic Church and it was hoped that some of them would become nuns. They had great admiration for the nuns who were their teachers. For this reason, and the fact that it was the only opportunity open to her, Marie, the first rebel, entered a strict religious order on November 19, 1953. Becoming a postulant with the

Servants of the Blessed Sacrament in Quebec City, Marie joined other members whose daily duty was round-the-clock prayer. The only time the nuns were permitted to speak was for a brief period after dinner and supper. This was a noble undertaking and Marie was sincere in her desire to become a nun, but it was hardly conducive to fulfilling herself as a person.

Emilie died alone in a convent. Shortly after the Quints left the Nursery and entered the Big House, Emilie began having attacks of epilepsy. The family considered this illness a shame to be guarded as a secret and she never received proper medical attention nor the drugs that could have aided her. The other Quints had always provided for her when she suffered the attacks, which became more violent and frequent as she entered adolescence. When she entered the "Home of the Happy Welcome," a convent to train workers who operated residences for elderly clergy, at Ste. Agathe, Quebec, the Order was not informed of her problem. (James Brough reported in *The Ladies' Home Journal* in 1974 that another reason for Emilie's entering the convent was to escape the sexual advancements of a relative.)

On the morning of August 6, 1954, Emilie was found face down in her bed, smothered to death. She had suffered a serious epileptic attack while the other nuns were attending Mass, and had turned over on her cot, becoming asphyxiated by the bedding. The other Quints were justifiably bitter over this needless loss. Emilie is buried in a small, lonely fenced-in cemetery at the back of a cow pasture in Corbeil where she gained worldwide attention with her birth only twenty years earlier. Among the condolences received were those of the eleven-year-old Diligentis, two boys and three girls from Buenos Aires, the only known surviving quintuplets in the world at that time.

Marie was at home with her parents when Emilie died. She had not been able to withstand the physical strain in her convent; and although she had been accepted as a novice, she left and returned to Corbeil, having no where else to go. Marie entered another convent later, but again poor health required hospitalization. She was informed by the Mother Superior that she could not return, so she decided to go into business for herself.

She rented a storeroom in Montreal and opened a flower shop, the Salon Emilie, a memorial to her sister. Papa Dionne would not hear to advancing any capital from Quintuplet funds for the venture; so by borrowing and applying for credit, Marie operated the Salon Emilie for six months until it failed. One reason for failure was Marie's generosity with customers and charities.

When the four surviving Quintuplets reached their twenty-first birthday in 1955, they received a reported one-fifth share of their million dollar trust fund. They then began, for the first time, to make their own decisions. They wore different clothes and each one had her hair fixed differently.

Illustration 40. Pictured with their parents as they graduated from high school, June 1952. *King Features.*

Illustration 41. Marie in 1952. *King Features.*

Yvonne and Cécile were training as nurses in a Montreal hospital and Annette was studying music at College Marguerite Bourgeois in Nicolet, Quebec. Marie was at this time still in the convent.

Marie and Annette later rented an apartment in Montreal, making a home for themselves and the other two sisters. Understandably, the girls wanted a life of their own. It was because of this newfound independence that in late 1955 Oliva Dionne, their father, called a press conference at the mansion in Corbeil, which had been built with Quintuplet funds and issued the statement:

Illustration 42. Top left. The four surviving Quints in The Salon Emilie, Marie's Flower Shop in Montreal, before their 22nd birthday. Left to right: Annette, Yvonne, Cécile and Marie. *International News Photos.*

Illustration 43. Top right. In memory of beloved Emilie, May 1955. Left to right: Marie, Yvonne, Cécile and Annette. *International News Photos.*

"The Quints did not come home for Christmas. We didn't even receive a card from them. They didn't write; they didn't phone. We have realized for some months that they have been drifting away...We decided it would be better if we didn't try to camoufage things any longer."

Oliva blamed "intruders" for the problem. This public attention achieved the desired results. Yvonne explained, "We sent a Christmas card. Is it our fault if they didn't get it?" All the girls except Marie, who was ill, then traveled to Corbeil for New Year's Day, the traditional French-Canadian day for gift-giving, and reconciled with their parents for the news photographers.Oliva issued a new statement: "There was a misunderstanding somewhere and it has been ironed out."

Their childhood, which affected their later years, was bound to be abnormal from the beginning. It was always a combination of public display and private seclusion. The Quints seldom left their home and when they did, it was generally under close supervision. They had no real friends and grew up to be introverts, depending only on each other. Beside Dr. Dafoe, the only personal contacts they ever had were the immediate family, nurses, nuns and priests. They were not permitted to be kissed when they were young, for fear of contracting germs; later when they were "reunited" with their parents, they were told that it was their "duty" to love and kiss them. After years of virtual bondage, they cherished their independence. They wanted friends their own ages—of both sexes—and they wanted a "normal life."

Papa Dionne was right. There were "intruders." Three of these intruders married Cécile, Marie and Annette. It looked as if for the first time these three could live ordinary lives, but it did not work out. Their backgrounds had permanently precluded any chances of success. All of the husbands for whatever their motives, contacted the girls "out of the blue" and they were the first outside men they had ever known. And each of them married the first man that she met.

Cécile met Phillipe Langlois because he read in the newspaper that she was a student nurse at Hôpital Notre Dame de l'Esperance in Montreal and called her on the phone and asked for a date. When it was announced that Cécile would marry the Quebec television technician, he became a celebrity and was invited to New York to appear on the popular television program *To Tell the Truth*. He preferred a rather ostentatious wedding ceremony and Cécile went along with it. They became the parents of five children, one of whom was a twin who was born severely deformed and who died at the age of fifteen months. Cécile slowly came to the realization that her marriage was not what she had hoped it would be. She and Langlois were permanently separated and she returned to nursing.

Illustration 44. The Quints leaving home after their 21st birthday in May 1955, wearing individual outfits of their own choice. Left to right: Marie, Yvonne, Annette and Cécile. *International News Photos.*

Illustration 45. Top left. Christmas 1955, after the "misunderstanding, in which the parents did not receive a Christmas card. Seated, left to right: Annette, Papa, Cécile. Standing: Mama and Yvonne. *International News Photos.*

Illustration 46. Top right. Cécile and her fiancé, Philippe Langlois.

Illustration 47. Bottom right. Cécile, left, and Yvonne when they graduated from nursing school at Notre Dame De l'Esperance Hospital in Montreal, September 8, 1957.

Cécile had been introduced to Germain Allard by another girl while she was in nurse's training. She already had a boyfriend, so she, in turn, introduced the college student to her sister Annette. Germain was very good looking and very ambitious. He and Annette were married on October 11, 1957, a few weeks before Cécile's wedding took place. By 1962 Annette had given birth to three healthy sons, but she became more and more disillusioned with her marriage. By 1974 she and Germain Allard were legally separated.

Marie also met her husband by chance. Florian Houle came to the church as a sightseer the day that Annette was married. He was a provincial government clerk who also lived and worked in Montreal and he attended the same church as Marie. He presented himself to Marie, and they were married within a year. She was twenty-four and Mr. Houle was forty-three. Marie also married the first man she had known. To avoid the wrath that her father had demonstrated at the other two engagements, she had not notified the family until after she was married in a private ceremony.

After several miscarriages, on Christmas Eve of 1960 Marie gave birth to another memorial to her sister Emilie, a baby girl named after her. Another daughter Monique, was born on June 7, 1962. Because of ill health and the fact that her husband's job required travel, Marie placed her children in foster homes and in 1966 became separated from him. It seems Marie lost interest in life.

Marie, who had been the most assertive, the most vivacious of the Quints, now remained in her apartment alone, neglecting to care for herself and not even bothering to eat. On February 27, 1970, her brother-in-law, Germain Allard, went to her apartment in Montreal with a policeman and broke down the door when she did not answer. Allard was concerned because he usually spoke with her by phone every day and had not heard from her over the weekend. Marie Houle had been dead for three days.

She was found face-down on the bed, the same way that Emilie had died. Marie was buried in St. Bruno, Quebec, a suburb of Montreal. Marie, always the most delicate Quint, the one who from birth was the most frail and later as an adult the one most susecptible to nervous conditions; the one who was born with a blood tumor on her leg; and the one who was described by admirers of the Quints as the "prettiest", had officially died of a blood clot in her heart. Marie's funeral was the first occasion on which the surviving Quints and their parents had been together since Cécile's wedding in 1957.

Yvonne is the only one of the Quints who has never married. As a child she was called the "natural leader" of the girls. It was probably Yvonne who developed the strongest personality. She left the Corbeil mansion when she was twenty, never to return, and entered the College Marguerite Bourgeois in Montreal to enroll in art courses. Her paintings and wood carvings were described as being above amateur standing Yvonne also completed nurse's training, and like Marie entered a convent. She served in convents longer than Emilie or Marie had, and intended to devote her life to caring for handicapped children. Yvonne, the most restless, most artistic and most intellectual of the Quints, was invited to leave the convent by the Little Franscian Sisters at Baie St. Paul when they realized that she would never be happy with their way of life.

Today Yvonne seems to be the most adjusted of the Quints. Her life, never having married, has been different than that of her sisters, but she was exposed to more experiences. She continued to study art and spent several summers traveling abroad. She works in the municipal library in St. Bruno and lives alone there in an apartment near the other surviving Quints.

The birthdays of the Quints are no longer a celebration. Since the death of Emilie in 1954, they have not been in close contact with their family. They are surely no longer bitter over their "side show childhood" and have learned to live with, and to understand somewhat the exploitation, the public quarrels, and the unhappiness that resulted from what was supposed to be a joyful reunion with their family, when they were seven years old. The words of bitterness that have been printed in countless newspaper columns since the Quints revealed their childhood misery to *McCall's Magazine* in 1963 have left their toll on the Dionne parents who never deliberately intended to treat them wrongly. Family relations will no doubt always be cool. Less attention has been given to the happy experiences of the Big House. There were fun and games shared with their brothers and sisters on the property in summer and in snow; the shopping excursions into North Bay or Callander,

without supervision and without all five being along; they enjoyed films and local events and other incidental pleasures which were not different than those experienced by other youngsters in the community. It was their fame that prevented them from being free.

McCall's Magazine of February 1964 carried the feature "Four Dionnes Write an Open Letter To Five Fischers" in which advice was offered to North America's newest residents of "Quintland." They advised the family of the Fischers, based upon their own traumatic experiences as famous children. They told how families of quintuplets "face a test of the human spirit". They "exploded the myth" of the Dionnes, not to hurt anyone, but in hope the truth would be beneficial to the Fischers and to their children. They resented the deception of all the publicity, the endorsements and the exploitation of their childhood. They said that "Quintuplets seem to bring out the best and the worst in people" and that they were quickly marketed for a fast profit because nobody expected them to survive long enough to exploit all lucrative commercial opportunities. All of the circumstances that the Dionnes resented were those that also insured their survival; the problem was that they did not find happiness from it.

There are only three of them now. They are still alike physically, but each is a separate individual, a distinct personality, who is free to dictate her own destiny. They were plunged into adulthood, all at once when they were twenty, after a lifetime of being protected and after having no

Illustration 48. Bottom left. Annette with her husband Germain Allard and their second son, May 21, 1961.

Illustration 49. Bottom right. One of the last portraits of the four surviving Dionne Quintuplets, December 1965. Left to right: Cécile Langlois, Annette Allard, Marie Houle and Miss Yvonne Dionne.

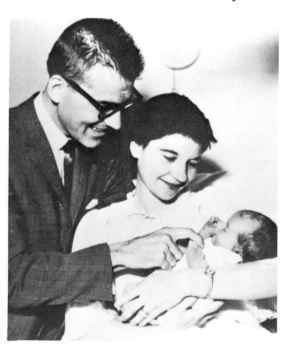

preparation for it. They are unable to forgive their parents for refusing to solicit medical attention for Emilie and for sending her to a convent to rest, which was no cure for epilepsy.

Emilie's death was a senseless waste and it was in no way her own fault. Marie did not have the apparent strength of Yvonne. Annette and Cécile are still the victims of a life that did not equip them to accept and understand intimacy, although they have the consolation of their own children.

Oliva and Elzire Dionne are still living within yards of the site where the Quints were born in Corbeil, where their married life began more than fifty years ago.

The humble Dionne family and its descendents will always be news and they will always be remembered because there *were* five of them who *were* all alike. The Dionne Quintuplets are still the only identical set the world ever saw and for this reason alone history will never forget them.

Illustration 50A. Left. Folder of the C & B Transit Co., "the Line of Friendlier Service." This is the 1938 Time Table for the steamer *City of Erie* which operated between Cleveland and Buffalo. Notice how the proposed route on the map crossed Lake Erie from Cleveland and showed the highway system north to Callander. Fares to cross the lake were $2.00 one-way and $4.00 roundtrip between Cleveland and Port Stanley; on weekends the fares were $3.50 going on Friday and returning Sunday. Staterooms were $2.00 one-way, luncheon was 75 cents and dinner was $1.00.

Illustration 50B. Below. The most popular photograph of the Dionne Quintuplets was this one taken in 1935. It was tinted in color, printed in many different sizes and was sold already framed. Oliva Dionne sold this picture at his souvenir booth. The babies, from left to right are: Yvonne, Annette, Cécile, Emilie and Marie.

II. North To Callander

By the summer of 1935 the tourist pilgrimage to northern Ontario had begun. Most news copy referred to Callander as the home of the Quints, although the site of the Dionne farm would pertain more to the village of Corbeil as the parish church is located there. Advertising data also credited Callander, and sometimes North Bay, the largest town in the Lake Nipissing region, as the "home of the Dionne Quintuplets."

Tourist agencies furnished motorists with plans on how to arrive at the east shore of Lake Nipissing so that they could see the Quints in person. The government of Ontario printed photographs of the Dionne babies and built up the Nipissing district as a vacation wonderland in their yearly travel guide booklets. And the visitors poured in with savings to spend in "Quintland." 1938 was one of the best years. An estimated 100,000 visitors left more than a million dollars in Ontario that summer.

Who of these lucky vacationers could possibly return home without some souvenir of the Dionne Quintuplets? Even *The North Bay Nugget* printed a special "Quintuplet Edition" of the area newspaper each summer which sold for 10 cents.

The North Bay area was severely hit by the Depression and was falling into bankruptcy before the Quints were born. Because of the Quintuplet industry, the entire region enjoyed prosperity by 1938 and boasted new buildings, where the old ones had been falling into disrepair. Tourists brought money. The Quintuplets were a "family attraction." An attraction that brought out the entire family was one that earned more money. Everyone associated with the tourist business knew that with women along more money would be spent. The home of the Quints was more than 300 miles from the nearest American border and most automobile trips from the United States were ones of at least 1,000 miles. This was a major journey for travelers in the 1930s. They would spend the money and worry about it later. In those "hard times" people did not feel that it was "wrong" to spend what little cash they had on an event as innocent as a visit to the Quints, combining it with a quiet vacation in rural Canada. All over the area there were souvenir shops, hot dog stands, refreshment booths and hundreds of places to stay overnight, including "Kwint Kabins."

The most famous of the shops were those of the Midwives Madame Legros and Madame Labelle located near Dafoe Hospital and that of Oliva Dionne across the road near his own home. After people saw the Quints in person they were eager to open their purses and empty their pockets. Even when the awe and inspiration wore off they never regretted owning a memento of the occasion. A large sign in 1936 tempted visitors with "Friends! We offer for sale a beautiful six colored framed picture of our Quintuplet Babies. These pictures are boxed for safe carrying and each one is autographed by Mrs. Dionne and myself. Oliva Dionne. Price $1.50." After all, they bought it from the father of the Quintuplets himself! He was as important as any movie star!

A visitor also stood the chance of picking up firsthand gossip to relate to those back home. The trips to Quintland were discussed and reported for years. It was worth every hard-earned dollar spent in Canada. The place where the Quints lived behind high fences, surrounded by policemen and guards, was a virtual concentration camp; but visitors always remembered it as something wonderful.

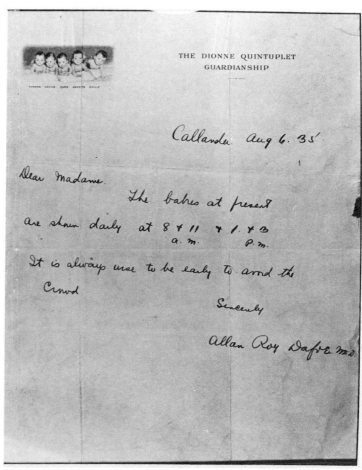

Illustration 51. An original letter handwritten by Dr. Allan Roy Dafoe in response to an anticipated visit to the home of the Quints. Those who remember "the crowd" report that it was the fullest early in the morning, long before the gates opened, contrary to Dafoe's advice.

Afternoon Crowds to see the Dionne Quintuplets, Callander, Canada. 2.
La foule qui se rend chaque après-midi pour voir les enfants, Callander, Canada.

Illustration 52. Postcard from Callander.

Illustration 53. The gates of Quintland have been opened for the afternoon crowd. The fleetest of foot were able to line up first for the one-way glass hallway that surrounded the playing yard of the Quintuplets. Children and well-dressed matrons alike show their enthusiasm with flying feet. The souvenir stand operated by "Madam Legros and Madam Lebel," the midwives who delivered the first three Quints, would be visited later for mementos of the living history that had been seen firsthand.

Visitors watching the Dionne Quintuplets, Callander, Canada.—7.
La parade des quintuplettes que la foule attend avec impatience.

Illustration 54. Postcard from Callander. The babies were not always kept behind one-way glass so that they would be "un-aware" of the curious stares of visitors. Sometimes the fortunate, especially in bad weather, could see them closely as they lined up on the porch of Dafoe Hospital to sing simple French-Canadian folk tunes.

Madame Legros' with the original Basket and Basin used for the Quints, Callander, Canada

THE ORIGINAL BASKET IN WHICH THE QUINTUPLETS WERE PLACED AFTER BIRTH

THE BASIN WHICH WAS USED FOR

Illustration 55. Madame Legros from a postcard that she sold at her souvenir stand. For 25 cents visitors could purchase the booklet "Administering Angels of the Dionne Quintuplets." The pamphlet was subtitled, "A true story of the birth of the Dionne Quintu-plets, as told by Madame Legros and Madame Labelle, midwives for the Dionne Quintuplets." Mrs. Donalda Legros was a cousin of Mrs. Dionne by marriage and she entered the practice of midwivery in 1917 at the age of 27. Mrs. Labelle, the other midwife who had attended Mrs. Dionne in the birth of the Quints and in two previous confinements entered her profession at the age of 47, ten years earlier. She was the mother of eighteen children and had assisted in about 300 births, although she reported that she had been paid for only twenty-five of them. The average fee was a little over a dollar. (Madame Labelle was not consistent in the spelling of her name.)

In the 1950s Madame Legros was still operating a shop based on her fame with the Quintuplets. She had relocated in Callander where she continued to advertise "the original basket of the Quints" although Oliva Dionne claimed that he had given her a duplicate basket and Dr. Dafoe stated that he had burned the original one. In the 1930s three different curio shops were displaying the "authentic and original basket" in which the Quints were placed after birth.

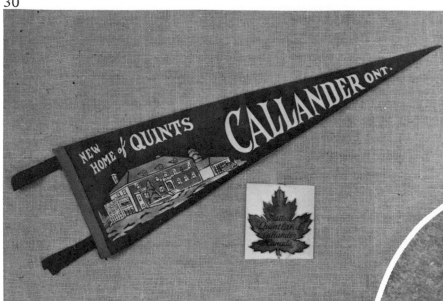

Illustration 56 & 57. Typical souvenirs from the shop of Madame Legros. The spoons with Canada's maple leaf symbol measure about 4 inches. The pennant is 22-1/2 inches long.

Illustration 58. A souvenir of Callander, which took credit as being the home of the Quints, because it was the home of Dr. Dafoe. It is a wooden display item with photographs of the Quints behind a celluloid protector. *Lois Barrett Collection.*

Illustration 59. Oliva Dionne, the father of the Quints, operated his own souvenir pavilion on his property. He and Mrs. Dionne autographed pictures and calendars, for a small fee, in the presence of memento purchasers. One of the best selling items was the famous "fertility stones" or "passion pebbles." When it was noticed that visitors picked up rocks from the property as souvenirs or good luck charms, Oliva realized that he was well-stocked with these items and that there was no overhead to maintain. He simply sold stones from his property. His land was extremely rocky and this was the most profitable thing it produced. Mr. Dionne did not market the stones as having any special powers. Newsmen gave him the publicity free. The rock pictured was purchased by a friend from Oliva Dionne in August 1938 and cost $1.00. It weights 1-1/2 pounds and measures about 2-1/2 inches by 5 inches. Smaller versions sold for 50 cents.

Illustration 60. Dionne Quintuplet souvenirs were marketed all over the touristic areas of Canada during the late 1930s and early 1940s. This linen baby's bib has the likenesses of the Quints stamped on it in blue. The same shade is used for the border and the ties. On the bottom portion the word Canada and the design around it are embroidered in the same color. It measures 8-3/4 inches by 11 inches and has been kept in like-new condition over the years.

Illustration 62. A cake plate that is stamped "Niagara Falls" in gold. It is heavy china and measures 11-1/2 inches from top to bottom. The photograph of the Quints is in color and the band around the plate is red. *Marge Meisinger Collection.*

Illustration 61. A dime and a penny were placed in a machine so a person could make their own souvenir. By pulling on a lever the penny was pressed into a flat medal showing the Quintuplets. The back side of this medal is plain, but different machines produced different versions of a similar medal. *Marge Meisinger Collection.*

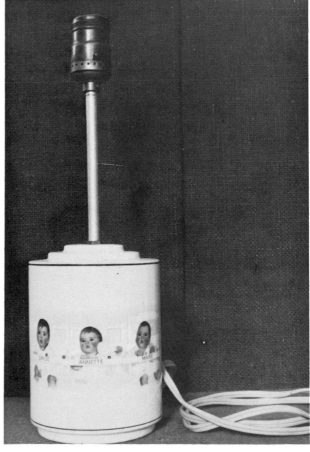

Illustration 63. 7-1/4 inch diameter china plate. The same pictures are used and the coloring matches the larger plate. Obviously different plates were available so that a purchaser would want a set on which all the Quints were pictured. *Marge Meisinger Collection.*

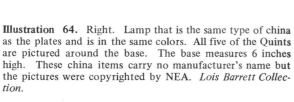

Illustration 64. Right. Lamp that is the same type of china as the plates and is in the same colors. All five of the Quints are pictured around the base. The base measures 6 inches high. These china items carry no manufacturer's name but the pictures were copyrighted by NEA. *Lois Barrett Collection.*

Illustration 65. Those who could not get to **Quintland** could purchase Quint treasures through the mail or buy them locally. Daniel Low & Co. of Salem, Massachusetts, offered charms and bracelets on which to wear them. The Quints Home, no. P382, sold for 50 cents and the Quints Tub, no. P383, sold for 25 cents. A bracelet, no. P381, included three gold-plated charms—a heart, a picture of the Quints and their bed—and sold for $1.00. The "Dionne Bows" (pictured) is a gold-colored metal bow that is constructed so that the clasp holds satin ribbons. The front, measuring 3/4·inches by 7/8 inches, is imitation mother-of-pearl and is set like a brooch. *Marge Meisinger Collection.*

Illustration 66. Card that held five pink satin hairbows. John C. Welwood Corp., N.Y.

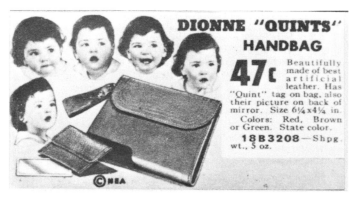

Illustration 67. 1 inch by 1-3/8 inch clasp from a purse. The color picture under celluloid is set on a gold-colored metal backing. The purse was a "leather-like" material and was silk lined. It measured 3-1/2 inches by 6-1/4 inches and came in a choice of red, blue, green or brown for $1.15. Like the bow and handbag, the picture would date it about 1936. *Connie Chase Collection.*

Illustration 68. Ad from "Sears Specials for Winter and Christmas 1936." *Marge Meisinger Collection.*

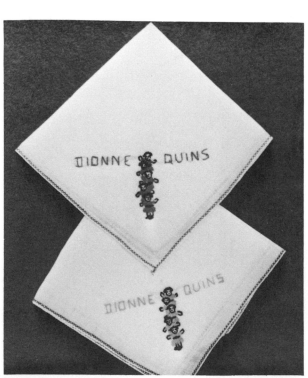

Illustration 69. Loraine Burdick's pioneer works, the *Celebrity Doll Journal*, tells of Quint dresses, sweaters and coats marketed in 1936. In 1937 Sears catalog offered Quint handkerchiefs. The fancier ones cost three for 19 cents and the plain printed ones sold at six for 29 cents. These two are white; one is embroidered in green, the other in blue. 8-1/4 inches by 8-1/4 inches. *Marge Meisinger Collection.*

Illustration 70. 8-1/2 inch by 8-1/2 inch cotton handkerchief in color. The background is red and the pictures of the Quints are black and white with blue in their dresses. This product, like most depicting the Quints, was copyrighted by NEA. *Marge Meisinger Collection.*

Illustration 71A. These two items were sold as practical accessories originally; now they are Dionne Quintuplet Collectibles in the collection of Jimmy and Fay Rodolfos. The cotton handkerchief measures about 9 inches by 9 inches. The label in the dress reads: "Size 1. By appointment to the Dionne Quintuplets exclusive licensee." It was once worn by some little girl who could "dress like the Quints." *Photograph courtesy of Jimmy and Fay Rodolfos.*

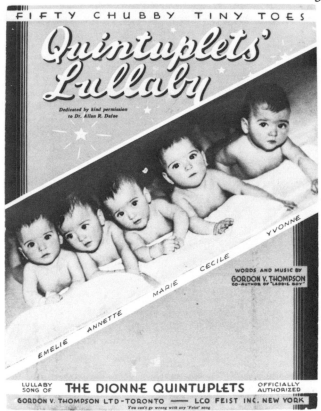

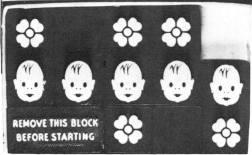

Illustration 71B. Loraine Burdick reports that all sorts of toys and games were manufactured using the name Dionne or capitalizing on their fame and referring only to "Quintuplets." There were tablets, coloring books, leather marble bags, bubble pipes, toy dishes, sewing kits, plaster craft kits and everything else imaginable. This is a puzzle, made like dominos, in a cardboard box. The object was to slide the pieces around until the "Quinties" were lined up. (One piece is missing.) There was no reference to the Dionnes in this unauthorized game from the Embossing Company, Albany, New York. The game is No. 3520 and the box measures 3-1/2 inches by 5-1/2 inches.

Illustration 72A. In 1935 non-travelers could play the *Quintuplets' Lullaby* on the piano. This is one of two different songs inspired by the Quints. The rotogravure section of Sunday newspapers on December 15, 1935, showed several pictures of dancer Dixie Dunbar who demonstrated "The Dionne Walk," a new tap dance routine based on a quintuple tap. *Marge Meisinger Collection.*

Illustration 72B. This Stewart-Warner table radio was manufactured about 1939. It was endorsed by, and depicts the Dionne Quintuplets, in applied color decals. The heavy plastic case measures about 9-1/2 inches long by 4-1/2 inches high. The radio is still in good working order, never having been repaired. A different Stewart-Warner radio is pictured on page 130.

Real wrist watches, the finest Christmas presents any girl or boy wants. Accurate timekeepers with attractive non-tarnishing cases that look like white gold and with the newest metal wristbands. Either is a present every girl or boy should have when so easy to earn. Unbreakable crystals, silver dials and black numbers. Guaranteed. Gift No. 455D (at right) for three or more subscription orders amounting to only $3. Gift No. 560D (smaller and daintier case, at left) for four or more subscription orders amounting to only $4.

The ever-popular clamp seal cooker which prepares a whole delicious meal without pot watching. Here is a real kitchen help. Meat and potatoes may be cooked in the bottom with a vegetable, pudding or sauce in the inset pan. You visit, go to church, or busy yourself in other parts of the house while your cooker takes care of the meal. Pure aluminum with 2 large green shakers included. Gift No. 502D for two or more subscription orders amounting to only $2.

Get This Extra Present

50 Christmas seals, tags, and cards will be included with any of the other presents that you earn if your subscription orders are for people living on a rural or star route and you give the route number with your order. Each piece in the big assortment is embossed in brilliant colors and is just what you need to wrap and send your Christmas gifts. You must hurry to win this for this offer is good before Christmas only.

Enjoy dinner parties with the Quins. Get this fascinating dinner set with Dionne Quins pictures--complete service for 6 including plates, cups, saucers, knives, forks, and spoons, paper napkins with pictures of the Quins and a real percolator that holds a pint--45 pieces in a beautiful picture box. All pieces made of rust-proof, sanitary, sparkling Mirro aluminum. Gift No. 662D for two or more subscription orders amounting to only $2.

Send your orders to
The FARMER'S WIFE Magazine
St. Paul, Minnesota

Illustration 73. Dionne Quins Mirro Aluminum 45-piece toy set. *The Farmer's Wife Magazine* offered this as a Christmas gift in December of 1936 for "two or more subscription orders amounting to $2." *Marge Meisinger Collection.*

Illustration 73A. A quality item that was inspired by the Famous Five is this clock made of pot metal painted a brass color. It measures about 2-3/4 inches by 5 inches and is still in working order. On the back of the clock it is embossed.
LUX CLOCK MFG CO. WATERBURY, CONN. U.S.A. The embossing on the bottom reads:
F.P. DRESSLER N.Y.
MADE IN U.S.A.
Jimmy and Fay Rodolfos.

Illustration 73B, C, & D. Three unauthorized quintuplet toys that no doubt sold very well. *Can You Feed the Quintuplets?* is a picture of five identical babies in a cardboard box, measuring about 3-1/2 inches by 7 inches, made by the Heininger Co., Orange, New Jersey. The "bottles" are celluloid capsules containing a lead weight that acts like a "Mexican jumping bean." The other game is *Quintuplets. Goo! Goo! Eyes!* and is about 3-5/8 inches by 5-1/8 inches in a metal frame with a glass front. Lead "beebies" act as eyes. The manufacturer is unknown. The baby buggy contains five tiny heads and is made of celluloid. There are no manufacturers marks on the 1-1/2 inch by 1-1/2 inch toy but an attached paper tag says that it is a "Souvenir of New York City." *Jimmy and Fay Rodolfos.*

Illustration 73E. Unauthorized items and "knock-off" items that related to the Quints are often more interesting and more uncommon than some of the "genuine" items. This lamp is an extremely rare Dionne Quintuplet Collectible from the collection of Jimmy and Fay Rodolfos and carries no Dionne endorsement. The statuary measures 11 inches high and is 10-1/2 inches across at the widest point. The eyes of the babies are painted blue on the chalkware figure and the doctor looks more like Mr. Dionne than he does Dr. Dafoe. On the back of the figure it is inscribed:

BREVETTE 1934

and there were no other sets of "5 Jumelles" (the French equivalent of Quintuplets) to inspire production at the time except the brown-eyed Dionnes. Also marked on the back of the lamp is the following, which signifies at least its place of origin:

PARFUMERIE SOUVENIR
STATION POSTALET
BOITE, 2
MONTREAL

Photograph courtesy of Jimmy and Fay Rodolfos.

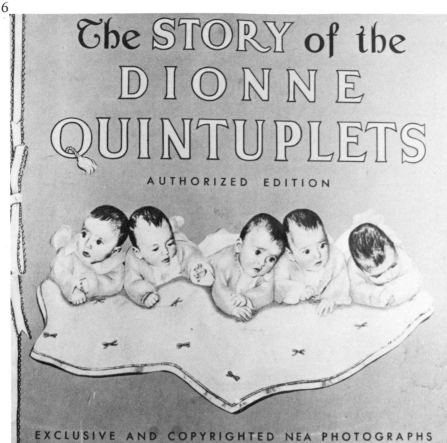

THE STORY of the
DIONNE
QUINTUPLETS

AUTHORIZED EDITION

EXCLUSIVE AND COPYRIGHTED NEA PHOTOGRAPHS

Illustration 74. Not only were there pictures of the Quints in the newspapers almost daily, but booklets full of photographs of the Dionnes with a color cover were marketed on a regular basis. These paperbound booklets sold for 10 cents in the 1930s. Today at flea markets they sell from $5.00 to $10.00, depending on their condition. The cover titles of the booklets show how frequently they came out in the early years. Whitman Publishing Company. 1935; 40 pp. 9-1/8 inches x 9-7/8 inches.

The DIONNE
QUINTUPLETS
We're Two Years Old

Illustration 75. Whitman Publishing Company, 1936; 40 pp. 9-1/8 inches by 9-7/8 inches.

Illustration 76. Dell Publishing Company, Inc., 1936; 32 pp. 8-1/2 inches x 9-3/4 inches.

Illustration 77. Whitman Publishing Company, no. 970, 1936; 32 pp. 9-1/2 inches by 10 inches. *Lois Barrett Collection.*

Illustration 78. Left. Whitman Publishing Company no. 975, 1937; 32 pp. 9-1/2 inches by 10 inches. *Lois Barrett Collection.*

Illustration 79. Right. Dell Publishing Company, Inc., 1936 36 pp. 8-1/2 inches by 9-3/4 inches.

Illustration 80. Left. Clothbound book of 62 pages, measuring 8-1/2 inches by 11 inches. The Platt and Munk Company, Inc., 1935. This book was copyrighted by Stephen Sleisinger, Inc., New York, as are all the paperbound booklets, and like them, all photographs were by NEA. Inside the front cover Fred S. Ferguson, President of NEA Service, Inc., authored the following dedication:

To
Dr. Allan Roy Dafoe
&
Hon. David Croll
Minister of Welfare of Ontario
This book is dedicated

Then followed a long endorsement about Dafoe's and Croll's part in ensuring the "babies' welfare." (Guess who signed the NEA contracts?) *Marge Meisinger Collection.*

Illustration 81. This book is a first-grade primer and was copyrighted in the Philippine Islands. It was published by Thomas Nelson & Sons, New York, 1937. There are 229 different words employed in the text and each page carries a NEA photograph that is narrated. The author pointed out in a note to the teacher that "the girls are called 'quins' because the word *quintuplet* is a long one and hard to say." The chapters are "The Quins," "Fun in the Snow," "Fun in the House," "The Birthday," "Sunny Days" and "Thanksgiving and Christmas." The copyright information indicates that the book was used to teach English to Spanish-speaking children in the Philippines.

Illustration 82. The fortunate could watch the Quints over and over again on 16-millimeter home movies of Dupont safety film. (Movie film prior to this time was made of nitrate and was highly flammable.) The film is entitled *Day With Quints* and was marketed in 1938. *Marge Meisinger Collection.*

Illustration 83. Baby's records could be kept in a heavy paper booklet after 1935. One wonders how many babies in the late 1930s were compared with the Dionne Quintuplets in such records! There are pages for such things as "Baby's Pictures", "Baby's Bank Account" (by the month no less!), and pages with the "Quints' Weight Chart" on one side and "Our Baby's" on the other. Included also is such data as "Baby's Schedule," etc. 5-3/4 inches by 8-3/4 inches. *Marge Meisinger Collection.*

40

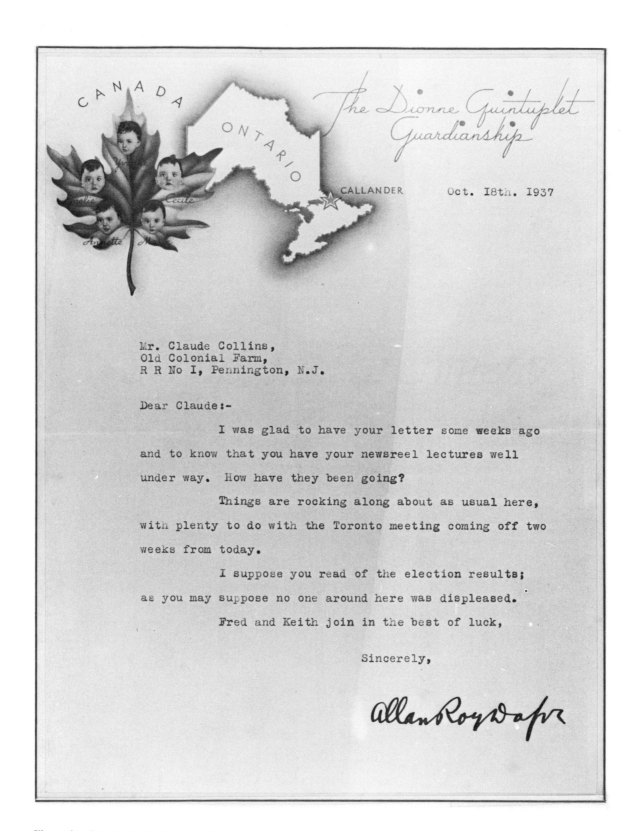

The Dionne Quintuplet Guardianship

CANADA · ONTARIO

CALLANDER   Oct. 18th. 1937

Mr. Claude Collins,
Old Colonial Farm,
R R No I, Pennington, N.J.

Dear Claude:-

     I was glad to have your letter some weeks ago
and to know that you have your newsreel lectures well
under way. How have they been going?

     Things are rocking along about as usual here,
with plenty to do with the Toronto meeting coming off two
weeks from today.

     I suppose you read of the election results;
as you may suppose no one around here was displeased.

     Fred and Keith join in the best of luck,

        Sincerely,

        Allan Roy Dafoe

Illustration 84. Original letter from Dr. Dafoe to Claude Collins, who was in charge of Dionne Quintuplet newsreel and home movie films for Pathé. Mr. Collins worked closely with the Doctor, as did Keith Munro, financial advisor for the Quints, and Fred Davis, the NEA photographer, both of whom are cited in this letter, which was typed by Dafoe's secretary.

III. Cover Girls

The Dionne Quintuplets have appeared on the covers of most American magazines. The cover was for a feature news story or for general articles about their upbringing and their development. These magazines sell today for $2.00 to $30.00 and are highly prized by collectors. In the appendix there is an extended bibliography of periodicals in which the Quints were featured. The magazines are cited as to covers, articles and advertising. This information can be useful to collectors who wish to locate magazines at flea markets or in used-book shops. Much of the credit for gathering this material goes to Marge Meisinger of Naperville, Illinois, whose movie magazine collection can not be found in any library.

Illustration 86. 1936. Painting by Earl Christy. *Marge Meisinger Collection.*

Illustration 85. The Quints' first cover. August 1935. The drawing was done by Maud Tousey Fangel. The Crowell Publishing Company of Springfield, Ohio, also furnished subscribers with a color print of this cover, suitable for framing, for 10 cents in stamps.

Illustration 87. 1936 Painting by Earl Christy. *Marge Meisinger Collection.*

LIFE

G ON THREE

MAY 17, 1937 10 CENT

Illustration 88. May 17, 1937. *Lois Barrett Collection.*

OVER 144 PAGES IN THIS ISSUE!

Modern Screen

APRIL
10
CENTS

THE LARGEST
CIRCULATION
OF ANY SCREEN
MAGAZINE

SHIRLEY TEMPLE
AND THE QUINTS

"I WANT TO PLAY WITH THE QUINTS," says SHIRLEY TEMPLE

Illustration 89. 1937. The Quints with Shirley Temple on a cover that no general magazine ever equalled for beauty. *Marge Meisinger Collection.*

Illustration 91. September 2, 1940.

Illustration 90. June 1940.

44

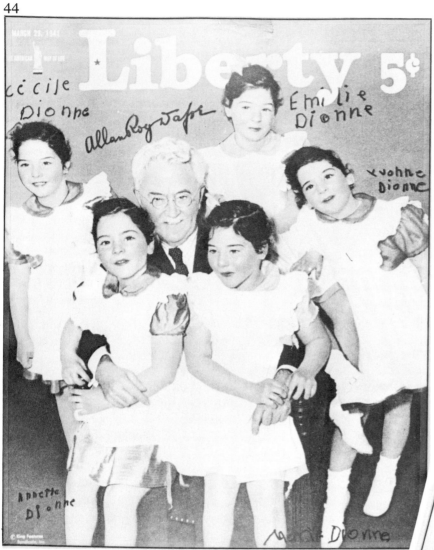

Illustration 93. March 29, 1941.

Illustration 92. October 14-18, 1940. *Marge Meisinger Collection.*

IV. "The Only One The Quints Use"

A great variety of products and items were endorsed by the Dionne Quintuplets. The contracts were first arranged by Dr. Dafoe and the guardians and later by Oliva Dionne, the girls' father. The Quints were always associated with "quality" products, never with inferior merchandise. But the Quints themselves were saved from the "taint of commercialism." There was no charge to see them and no charge for parking cars near their property. They only endorsed products that they themselves actually used in their daily lives. NEA printed billions of photographs of the Quints, both from Fred Davis' snapshots and from all the artists' renderings. These pictures were used on commercial items that the Quints did not endorse, but the items were given free to retail consumers in the United States.

At times consistent with their ages the girls endorsed Lysol disinfectant, Palmolive soap, Karo syrup, Colgate dental creme, Quaker Oats cereal, Baby Ruth candy bars, and a variety of other things that they probably did use. Irradiated Carnation Milk, "from contented cows," said in October of 1939 that it was "good for Quints, Quadruplets too, Triplets, Twins, or what have YOU!" Like many other products, Carnation took credit for being "...the same milk that helped the Dionne Quintuplets through many critical months." Colgate-Palmolive paid $55,000 to the Quintuplet account for endorsements over a three-year period and public approval of Quaker Oats made the Quints $25,000 richer, just to mention two products. This writer can remember using Karo syrup on everything edible as a child and has not been aware of its existence since. Many parents in the late 1930s and early 1940s felt they were not providing the best possible for their children unless they gave them the same products the Quints used.

The incident that throws the most light on the commercial significance of the Quintuplets was the prolonged legal battle between two Canadian manufacturers of corn syrup. When it was learned that the Quints' first meal was a 7-20 mixture of cow's milk and water with a few drops of rum and corn syrup added, the president of the St. Lawrence Starch Company, manufacturer of Beehive Syrup, rushed a case of the company's product north to Callander. A "goodwill" check arrived with the syrup and later company advertisements proclaimed the fact that Beehive Syrup had been the first food consumed by the celebrated sisters. Sales became so brisk that the company increased advertising from $12,000 in 1933 to $246,000 in 1936 – according to evidence that later came out in court.

Crown Brand Syrup from the Canada Starch Company had formerly been the leading national brand. The rival concern's sales fell off so sharply that they entered litigation against Beehive for $150,000 and asked for a court order to stop the Beehive promotion. The plaintiff contended that it was a known fact that there had been a can of Crown Brand Syrup in the Dionne kitchen during the birth of the Quints.

Months later, after the case had progressed through the Canadian courts, the judgment came out in favor of the defendant. Beehive won the field based on the evidence of Nurse Leroux who had given the 7-20 mixture to the babies. She swore–and Crown's lawyers were not able to shake her testimony under cross-examination–that the syrup she had used for the mixture suggested by Dr. Dafoe came in a can that carried the Beehive label.

The case was not a major precedent-setting one and was viewed as comedy from the beginning, but it did serve to emphasize the high regard in which the Quints were held by businessmen who knew that their product would be more marketable with an endorsement by the world's most famous babies.

And if the Quints' endorsement was not enough, most advertising carried a message by Dr. Dafore or Nurse Leroux and cited "medical evidence" as to the value of the product. It is ironic, though, that Dr. Dafoe autographed the advertisements for "first and only candy served the Quints" and said, "Baby Ruth, being rich in Dextrose, vital food-energy, sugar, and other palatable ingredients, makes a pleasant, wholesome candy for children." The Quints stated that they were denied candy in the Nursery, which they were told was bad for their teeth. This was one weapon that Mama Dionne used against Dafoe to gain the support of her children in the custody fight. And more ironically, the Baby Ruth ads were used in family magazines during the spring of 1941. This was when Dr. Dafoe resigned his position as the Quints' guardian.

All items that carried a picture of the Quints are now collectibles. So are the advertising data and product premiums.

Illustration 94. Deck of playing cards. 1936. The aces proclaim: "Use Hyred gasoline. It's Ethyliz-ed." *Connie Chase Collection.*

Illustration 95. Close-up of playing cards. The pic-ture of the babies in the basket is in full color. They are, from left to right, Marie, Cécile, Emilie, Yvonne and Annette. *Connie Chase Collection.*

Illustration 96. Double deck, showing the same picture. One set has a pink bor-der, the other is blue. The carton, like the single deck, has the girls' names around the outside edges. *Marge Meisinger Collection.*

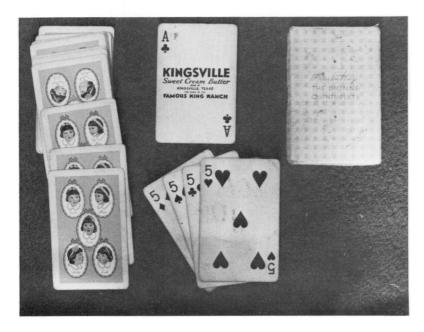

Illustration 97. Different deck of playing cards, also 1936. The picture of the girls is an artist's rendering and is tinted. The background is pink. This deck was a customer gift to promote butter from the King Ranch in Texas. *Marge Meisinger Collection.*

Illustration 98. Close-up of King Ranch deck. *Marge Meisinger Collection.*

Illustration 99. Cardboard fans on wooden handles. The fans varied slightly in shape from year to year, but are all about 8 inches by 15 inches. Left fan: "Sweehearts of the World," 1936; this is a photograph compilation. The right fan "Springtime," 1940 is from a painting by Andrew Loomis. The fans were manufactured by Brown & Bigelow of St. Paul, Minnesota, and many of them are the same pictures used on the yearly calendars, although the fans were distributed only prior to World War II. *Lois Barrett Collection.*

Illustration 100. Fans in *Marge Meisinger's* collection. They are also in color, with the exception of the one at the left, the first fan produced, which is sepia-tone. From left to right, clockwise, they are. "The Family Circle," 1935; "School Days," 1938; "Sweethearts of the World," 1936; 1937; and 1936. The last two fans are untitled and the dates refer to the copyright. Like the calendars, the fans probably came out the following year. The backs of these fans (in the same order) carry the firm name of the donor: Bert S. Gadd, Mortician, St. Paul Milk Company; Knutson Bros. Dairy, La Crosse, Wisconsin; Schmidt's Elkhorn Brand Ice Cream, Elkhorn, Wisconsin; and "If you like this fan, take it home." Krill's.

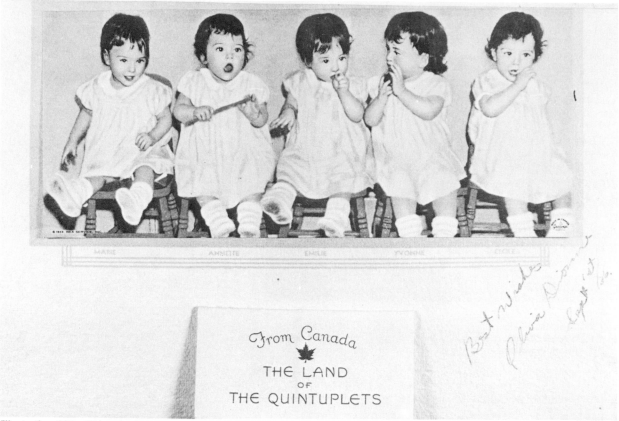

Illustration 101. This calendar was made in Canada by the Greetings Company, Toronto. It begins with September, 1936. It was autographed by Oliva Dionne on September 1, 1936, at the request of the lady who purchased it. On the back there is factual information about the birth of the Quints. It is also rubber-stamped in blue:

Souvenir	Corbeil, Canada
of Visit to Dionne	Purchased at
QUINTUPLETS	Booth Operated by QUINTS' PARENTS.

The NEA picture is dated 1936.

Illustration 102. 1936. The first of the Brown & Bigelow series. The photograph is from 1935. A printed sheet included with the calendar carries Quint information and statistics. *Lois Barrett Collection.*

The yearly Dionne Quintuplet calendars from Brown & Bigelow were distributed to dairies, grocery stores, and other retail establishments to be given out to customers at Christmas time. This was to remind them of the firm or the product, like the fans. The calendars are from the years 1936 to 1955, although the picture on it is always dated earlier. Brown & Bigelow calendars came in many different sizes and shapes, but each year's picture is usually the same. The pictures could also be ordered as prints, measuring up to about four feet wide, for framing.

THE *Dionne* QUINTUPLETS
Annette   Yvonne   Cecile   Marie   Emilie

THE CITY COAL & SUPPLY CO.
Phone 40197 — 1111 W. Rayen Ave.
Your Phone Call Starts Our Trucks

Illustration 103. Above. 1937. This is a painting based on a similar NEA photograph.

THE FIVE LITTLE SWEETHEARTS OF THE WORLD
Cecile   Yvonne   Marie   Emilie   Annette

Illustration 104. 1938. "The Five Little Sweethearts of the World." The Quints are, from left to right, Cécile as "Little Bo Peep;" Yvonne as "Little Miss Muffet;" Marie as "Mary Contrary;" Emilie as "Goldilocks;" and Annette as "Little Red Riding Hood." *Lorene Anderson Collection.*

Illustration 105. 1939. "Five Little Sweethearts–This Year They Are Five." The artist's signature on this calendar and the one from 1938 appears to be Elvgren. *Connie Chase Collection.*

THE DIONNE QUINTUPLETS
FIVE LITTLE SWEETHEARTS   THIS YEAR THEY ARE FIVE

THE DIONNE QUINTUPLETS—SCHOOL DAYS

Illustration 106.

1940. "School Days."

Illustration 107. 1942. "Springtime" is the title of the painting by Andrew Loomis. This year the Quints were eight years old. *Connie Chase Collection.*

Illustration 108. 1941. "All Dressed Up." The Quints, left to right: Annette, Cécile, Emilie, Yvonne and Marie. *Betty Cataldo Collection.*

Illustration 109. 1943. "Sunny Days" by Andrew Loomis. Left to right: Annette, Marie, Yvonne, Cécile and Emilie. *Lorene Anderson Collection.*

Illustration 110. 1944. "Maytime" by Andrew Loomis. Left to right: Annette, Cécile, Yvonne, Emilie and Annette. *Lorene Anderson Collection.*

52

Illustration 111. 1945. "Harvest Days" by Andrew Loomis.

Illustration 112. 1947. "Everybody Helps" by Andrew Loomis. The printing dates now begin to be two years earlier. *Connie Chase Collection.*

Illustration 113. 1946. "Queens of the Kitchen" by Andrew Loomis. Left to right: Cécile, Yvonne, Emilie, Marie and Annette. *Betty Cataldo Collection.*

Illustration 114. 1948. "First Dates" by Andrew Loomis. On the inside there is a dialogue for the painting: "Annette, at the phone, says, 'Quiet, girls I can't hear what he said...' Marie looks over the stair case [sic], hoping the call is for her. Yvonne, Emilie and Cécile crowd in close to hear the conversation. Soon their dates will be arriving—and each of the girls will have a corsage to add to their attractiveness." (Complete fiction!) *Connie Chase Collection. King Features Syndicate, Inc.*

YVONNE   ANNETTE   MARIE   CECILE   EMILIE
The Dionne Quintuplets   "FIFTEEN ALL"

Illustration 115. "Fifteen All" by Andrew Loomis. *Connie Chase Collection. King Features Syndicate, Inc.*

Illustration 116. 1950. "Sweet Sixteen" by Andrew Loomis. The girls never looked this glamorous in real life and the fiction continues on the inside page: "The girls love to ride and do so quite well. Wearing their bright red coats they are often seen on horseback in the beautiful country near the Dionne home. And so the artist has portrayed them." This collector does not believe that the Quints actually posed for any of the Loomis paintings, and this one and the following calendar covers help prove the point. *King Features Syndicate, Inc.*

Illustration 117. 1953. Painting by Andrew Loomis. 1953 is the year that Marie entered a convent. *Connie Chase Collection. King Features Syndicate, Inc.*

Illustration 118. 1951. "Out for Fun" by Andrew Loomis. *Connie Chase Collection. King Features Syndicate, Inc.*

Illustration 119. 1952. "Smooth Sailing" by Andrew Loomis. (This painting should have earned the Quints a lucrative Hollywood contract!) *Connie Chase Collection. King Features Syndicate, Inc.*

Illustration 120. 1954. "Landing Party" by Andrew Loomis. This happy summer scene of the Quints in a rowboat is ludicrous when one consideres that it was in August of 1954 that Emilie suffocated to death in a convent. *Connie Chase Collection. King Features Syndicate, Inc.*

Illustration 121. 1955. "Grown Up" by Andrew Loomis. The fictional painting was done two years previously and the calendar was printed at least a year earlier. Brown & Bigelow included an extra sheet with the calendar in a final tribute:

"As we distribute this, our final Dionne Quintuplet calendar, we share with you and the rest of the world our sorrow over the untimely death of Emilie last August.

Our picture of the Dionne sisters, in a happy mood, was painted for this calendar by Andrew Loomis at a time prior to Emilie's death when the circle was still unbroken. We issue it with the feeling that you many want to have and keep this copy of the last picture ever painted of the five girls whom the world took to its heart in Callander, Ontario, May 28, 1934, and has cherished as its own ever since."

Connie Chase Collection. King Features Syndicate, Inc.

American advertising wasted little time discovering the commercial value of the Quints. The advertising pages from magazines are now mounted in frames and are treasured collector's items. The premiums that were given free, or for a token price to cover mailing, are even more valuable. They are sought by collectors of the Dionne Quintuplets and by collectors of the articles that happened to be Quint-inspired, such as the Quintuplet spoons.

Illustration 123. "Protecting the Dionnes," a booklet of 24 pages giving hints for sanitation and cleanliness in raising babies. 1936, Lehn & Fink Products Corporation. Included are many NEA photos and Lysol ads. 5-1/4 inches by 8 inches. *Marge Meisinger Collection.*

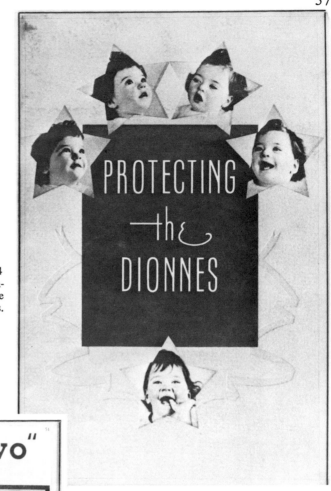

Five... "Going on Two"

The DIONNE QUINTUPLETS, now safely past that perilous first year

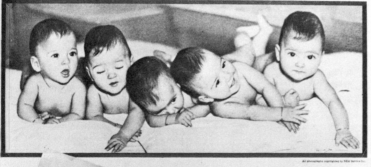

Since the day of their birth, "LYSOL" has been the only disinfectant used to help protect these famous babies from the constant dangers of infection

Illustration 122. Lysol advertising from the *Woman's Home Companion*, August 1935.

THE *Country Doctor* TALKS TO WOMEN

DR. ALLAN ROY DAFOE

Illustration 124. "The Country Doctor Talks to Women" by Dr. Allan Roy Dafoe. 1937, Lehn & Fink Products Corporation, 32 pages, 5-1/4 inches by 7-1/2 inches. This booklet on child care is "selected excerpts from Dr. Allan Roy Dafoe's radio talks, over the Columbia Broadcasting System's coast-to-coast network—as presented every Monday, Wednesday and Friday morning by 'Lysol' disinfectant—with the compliments of Lehn & Fink Products Corporation, Bloomfield, New Jersey." The "talks" were on the following subjects:

1. Sleeping habits
2. Feeding Habits
3. Cod Liver Oil Habit
4. Bath Habits
5. Tooth Brush Habit
6. Anti-Crying Habit

Dr. Dafoe tells how to discipline children, citing how he handled the Quints: "...Never punish them physically. They've never been spanked in their lives." If a Quint were being disciplined, the Doctor would "shut her up in a room...it is not dark... and let her cry until she sees that it doesn't pay."

7. Show-off Habit
8. Exercise Habits
9. The Cleanliness Habit
10. Routine Habit
11. The Examination Habit
12. The Happiness Habit

There are Lysol hints at the bottom of each page and one of them tells that "the first trained nurse to reach the Dionne home, when the Quints were born, had 'Lysol' in her kit and used it as a disinfectant." *Connie Chase Collection.*

Illustration 125. Karo syrup did not offer premiums to consumers, but their color ads are no doubt the most beautiful ones in which the Quints appeared. The girls were always referred to as the "Quints" in Karo advertising. *The American Magazine*, November 1937.

Illustration 126. The *Woman's Home Companion*, February 1937.

Illustration 127. *Modern Screen*, April 1937. *Marge Meisinger Collection.*

Illustration 128. Letter to Santa. Notice that Dr. Dafoe also signed the endorsement.

Karo is the only syrup served to the Dionne quintuplets. Its maltose and dextrose are ideal carbohydrates for growing children—

Allan Roy Dafoe, M.D.

Illustration 129. Karo ad that coincides with a holiday.

Illustration 130. *True Story*, February 1939.

Illustration 131. This 1940 series of ads featured paintings by Willy Pogany, an American artist who had been born in Hungary. On August 11, 1940, *The New York Times* reported that he would spend three months painting the portraits, after having completed his preliminary sketches in Corbeil. These same pages, with minor changes were also used for Kremel Dessert. *Good Housekeeping*, November 1940.

Illustration 132. Yvonne.

Illustration 133. Annette.

Illustration 134. Cécile.

Illustration 135. Emilie.

Illustration 136. Marie.

Why COLGATE DENTAL CREAM

IS DR. DAFOE'S CHOICE FOR THE DIONNE QUINS

80 baby teeth—kept pearly white with Colgate's!

A message of utmost importance TO EVERY MOTHER

WHO WANTS HER CHILDREN TO HAVE SOUND HEALTHY TEETH

THE Dionne Quintuplets! What babies were ever before raised with such scientific care! Always they have had the best of everything!

So, when the time came to choose a dentifrice for them, Dr. Dafoe chose Colgate Dental Cream . . . because Colgate's cleans so *thoroughly*, yet so *gently*—without the slightest harm to delicate enamel, or irritation to tender gums.

And how the Quins love Colgate's delightful peppermint flavor! Like all children, they really *enjoy* brushing their teeth with Colgate's . . . and what an important point this is in teaching correct habits of oral hygiene.

A LESSON FOR EVERY MOTHER!

As the specialists in charge of the Quins know so well, early dental care is so important! For the second or permanent teeth are formed in the jaw even before infancy. Thus, defects in the first teeth are communicated to the permanent teeth . . . affecting their color, shape, quality and position in the mouth. Defects in baby teeth may even affect the general health of the child.

So if you want your children to have fine, healthy teeth when they grow up, how wise you will be to follow Dr. Dafoe's example—and guard baby teeth with Colgate Dental Cream . . . make daily brushing with Colgate's a rigid rule!

IDEAL FOR ADULT TEETH, TOO

You will want to make Colgate's your toothpaste, too! Not only because its soft, safe polishing agent cleans the enamel to shining smoothness—but also because Colgate's special *penetrating* foam gets into all those tiny crevices between your teeth that ordinary cleansing methods fail to reach . . . cleans every surface of every tooth . . . keeps your breath beyond reproach!

COLGATE RIBBON DENTAL CREAM

20¢ LARGE SIZE
35¢ GIANT SIZE
OVER TWICE AS MUCH

Woman's Home Companion February 1937

Illustration 137. Colgate Dental Cream. *Woman's Home Companion,* February 1937. Colgate and Palmolive advertising always called the girls "Quins."

To guard their budding beauty

the Dionne Quins use only PALMOLIVE

the soap made with Gentle Olive Oil!

DR. DAFOE *Says:*

"At the time of the birth of the Dionne Quintuplets, and for some time afterward, they were bathed in Olive Oil . . . When the time arrived for soap and water baths, we selected Palmolive Soap exclusively for daily use in bathing their famous babies."

HOW adorable they are! Their great dark eyes, fringed with long, curling lashes . . . their rose-bud mouths!

No picture can do justice to these lovely Dionne Quins. For so much of their beauty is in their exquisite, baby-girl complexions . . . kept soft and smooth, both winter and summer, by Palmolive's gentle, protective care!

WHY THEY USE ONLY PALMOLIVE THE SOAP MADE WITH OLIVE OIL!

Because these famous little girls were born prematurely they have always had unusually sensitive skin. That is why, for sometime after their birth, they were bathed only with Olive Oil.

Dr. Dafoe, like doctors everywhere, knew that nothing is so soothing for delicate skin as gentle Olive Oil.

Then, when the time came for soap and water baths, how important it was to choose a soap made from the gentlest, most soothing ingredients! And so, Dr. Dafoe chose Palmolive, the soap made with Olive Oil, to be used exclusively for bathing the Quins' tender skin!

WHAT A LESSON FOR EVERY WOMAN!

Mother! Why should you risk bathing *your* precious baby, or any of your children, with any soap less gentle than the one chosen for the little Dionnes?

And you too, Lovely Lady . . . you who want to keep your complexion alluring through the years! Why not give *your* skin the beauty care that only Palmolive's secret blend of Olive and Palm Oils can give! Why not use safe, gentle, pure Palmolive for your own face and bath!

TO KEEP YOUR OWN COMPLEXION ALWAYS LOVELY, USE THIS BEAUTY SOAP CHOSEN FOR THE QUINS

Illustration 138. Palmolive Soap. Painting by Andrew Loomis. *Woman's Home Companion,* February 1937. Note Nurse Leroux's endorsement.

Illustration 139. Page ad from 1937. Painting of the Quints by Andrew Loomis. (This page alone cost $3.00 at a flea market.)

Illustration 140. Ad from the *Picayune New Orleans States Magazine*, August 1939. Each spoon was only 10 cents and the back wrapper from the cake of soap. This offer was not a lucrative one for Palmolive. "In the good old days" consumer product manufacturers offered a great variety of premiums that were free, or practically free. This was a form of advertising that has disappeared. Today advertising dolls and other toys and items sell for full value, and are just as desirable. Palmolive also offered free cutouts (pictured in chapter VI.) *Marge Meisinger Collection.*

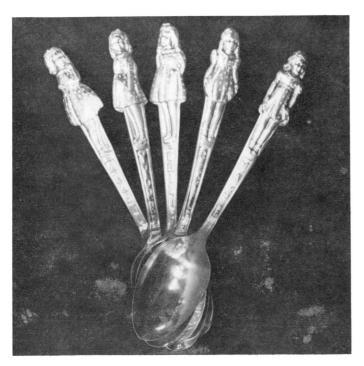

Illustration 141. Spoons from Palmolive. They are 6 inches long and are embossed "Carlton Silver Plate" on the back. Each of the Quints is depicted in a different pose and the reverse of the spoon shows her from the back. The order here, from left to right, is: Annette, Yvonne, Emilie, Cécile and Marie. The entire set cost 50 cents in 1939, today it would cost more than $50.00.

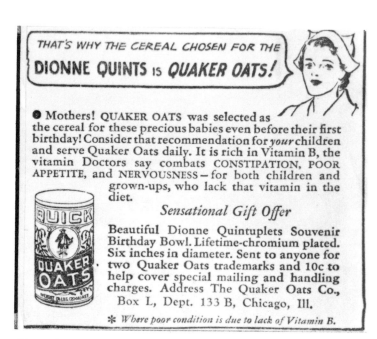

Illustration 142. Newspaper ad from November 1935 offering the Souvenir Birthday Bowl for only 10 cents.

Illustration 144. In 1935 and 1936 advertising from the Quaker Oats Company carried such slogans as "What Mother's Oats does for the Dionne Quins—it will do for you!" and "When the Dionnes' Doctor picked Mother's Oats, that's all we needed to know," and included photographs of a mother holding her baby next to the quote. The portion of the ad that carried a picture of the Quints (Quaker Oats also called them "Quins,") promised such things as "For a sweet nature like Marie's" eat Mother's Oats. Depending on the section of the United States, the cereal was sold as Quaker Oats or Mother's Oats. In some stores both brand names were stocked side by side. There was no difference between them. The ad pictured was from *Woman's Home Companion*, February 1937.

Illustration 143. Chrome-plated cereal bowl with the Quints pictured as babies in the bottom and their names inscribed around the rim. The bowl is actually 5-7/8 inches in diameter and 1 inch high.

Illustration 145. Ad from Sunday supplement of the newspaper, February 15, 1936. The text told readers to send for information on how to win a $10,000 "Dream Home." *Marge Meisinger Collection.*

Illustration 146. The contest entry form came in an envelope from the Quaker Oats Company, Chicago, Illinois. Contestants were instructed to write a letter of 100 words or less on the topic "Which of the Dionne Quins Would I adopt." Those who mailed their entry blank before March 31, 1936, the closing date, would receive a free 7 by 9 inch full-color photo of their favorite. *Marge Meisinger Collection.*

Marie Dionne

Illustration 147. Marie.

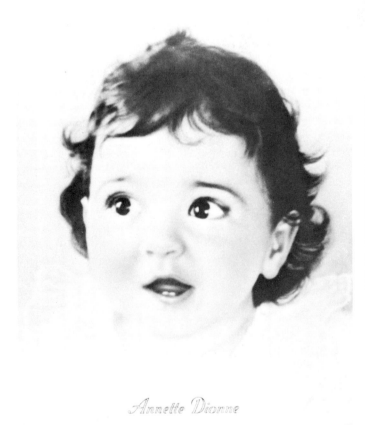

Annette Dionne

Cécile Dionne

Illustration 148. Annette. *Marge Meisinger Collection.*

Illustration 149. Cécile. *Marge Meisinger Collection.*

Illustration 150. Another Quaker Oats Contest in which entrants submitted a title for the picture of Dr. Dafoe with the Quintuplets. The entrant who submitted the most suitable name before October 30, 1936, would receive $12,340.25 in prizes; the most suitable name selected by the judges from those received between October 30 to December 15, 1936, would receive another $12,340.25 worth of "free gifts." The ad does not state what the free gifts were. From *Betty Cataldo's Scrapbook.*

Illustration 151. Left. Sanitized Mattress ad from Ward's Fall and Winter Catalog 1941-1942. "Sanitized Tickings...sold by mail only at Wards...are approved for use of the Dionne Quints by Dr. Allan Roy Dafoe and the Guardians." *Marge Meisinger Collection.*

Illustration 152. Label from a Sanitized Mattress in beautiful condition. It is presently being used by two-year-old Heidi Zimmerman. *Photo by Paul Zimmerman.*

THESE world-famous little ladies are certainly growing up in style • Here they're learning how the world's most famous motor car body has grown up, too—into the widest, longest, strongest Unisteel Turret Top Body by Fisher that General Motors cars have ever had • Its extra room, you can imagine, is a mighty important contribution to motoring comfort—while its newly strengthened steel construction makes your security on the highway more certain than ever • But of all the ultra-modern features with which the 1940 Body by Fisher abounds, none is more eye-opening than its Planned Vision • It increases the range of your view ahead with a wider windshield. It broadens your scope of traffic behind with a more effective placement of the rear-view mirror and a 10% to 18% larger back window. And it rids your sightseeing of distortion and eyestrain—by the use of genuine Safety *Plate* Glass all around • That's why you hear it repeated so often, "The buyword for '40 is Body by Fisher"—which means a General Motors car, of course.

Illustration 153. Fisher Body ad from *National Geographic*, April 1940. The pictures were "Copyright Dionne Quintuplets." This was after Dr. Dafoe had yielded the right to endorsements and contracts to Oliva Dionne.

V. Movie Stars

The Dionne Quintuplets appeared in three feature motion pictures for Twentieth Century-Fox. The films were *The Country Doctor* and *Reunion* in 1936 and *Five of a Kind* in 1938. The films were highly popular and profitable at the time they were released but they were never considered topnotch nor of great artistic merit. They were never revived later and they have not been offered for television viewing. The movies were made under the supervision of Darryl F. Zanuck and from all indications they were mounted strictly for profit.

At the time the motion picture contract was drawn up, the details that engendered the most interest and the most news copy were the prices that the Quints were paid for "acting" in the films. Their debut film *The Country Doctor* brought them $50,000. A short time later Mr. Zanuck, the head of the studio, presented them with an additional $250,000 for the rights to make three additional feature films. (Only two were made.) The contract called for an extra payment of $50,000 upon the completion of the three pictures, plus 10 percent royalties on all the profits from the films. This offer was the most lucrative one that the Quints had ever been offered.

The films were popular because the Dionne Quintuplets were so popular in the late 1930s, but they were far from being sophisticated productions. Canadians were offended by the way their country and their government were protrayed. The hometown of the "Country Doctor" was depicted as the "hinterlands" where disease epidemics were rampant, where government officials denied the population a decent hospital and where the local folk were well-meaning idiots. The first film contained a scene where an airplane left Montreal with serum in the middle of summer and arrived, with no delay, in the town representing Callander in the middle of winter.

All three films were fictionalized versions of the lives of the Dionne Quintuplets and Dr. Dafoe. The Dionnes were the Wyatt Quintuplets of Moosetown and John Qualen played their father Asa Wyatt. Qualen's characterization of a half-baked country bumpkin who climbed artificial trees to peek at his babies offended Mr. and Mrs. Dionne greatly. John Qualen played the father of the Quints with the same look of insipidity on his face that he employed as Muley in *The Grapes of Wrath*. When Asa told Nurse Kennedy (Dorothy Peterson) that although he had been a father six times already, he still got scared; she hastily replied with bitterness, "Yes, but not scared enough." Dr. Dafoe was pleased that his part was played by Jean Hersholt, who later had a long career on radio as "Dr. Christian." Hersholt, as Dr. Luke, was noble, sacrificing and dedicated to all the high values that Dafoe wanted to claim for himself. The plots were contrived by professional script writers and were mostly an excuse to present the Dionne Quintuplets to the public in movie theaters. Dr. Dafoe was the technical advisor and the Quints were photographed under his direction. Before this time Dafoe had never even heard of Greta Garbo and the only motion pictures he had seen were a newsreel of the Quints and a minor production called *Sunshine Susy*. Inspite of all advertising to the contrary, the Quints did not "act" in the Twentieth Century-Fox films. They played and frolicked and sometimes sang and all this was edited carefully so that it fit into the three stories.

But how collectors and film buffs would love **to see these films today!**

Illustration 154. Cover of the book *The Country Doctor* showing Jean Hersholt and the Dionne Quintuplets, Grosset & Dunlap, 1936. The first half of the book is a story based on the movie, the second half is "Five Little Dionnes and How They Grew." *Connie Chase Collection.*

THE COUNTRY DOCTOR

Story idea suggested by Charles E. Blake
Screenplay by Sonya Levien
Directed by Henry King
Produced by Darryl F. Zanuck
for
Twentieth Century-Fox

Roles:	Cast:
Dr. John Luke	Jean Hersholt
Mary MacKenzie	June Lang
Constable Jim Ogden	Slim Summerville
Tony Luke	Michael Whalen
Nurse Katherine Kennedy	Dorothy Peterson
MacKenzie	Rober Barrat
Mrs. Graham	Jane Darwell
Asa Wyatt	John Qualen
Dr. Paul Luke	Frank Reicher
Sir Basil Crawford	Mantagu Love
Governor General	David Torrence
Greasy	George Chandler
Mrs. Ogden	Helen Jerome Eddy
Mrs. Wyatt	Aileen Carlyle
Dr. Wilson	George Meeker
Mike	J. Anthony Hughes
The Gawker	William Benedict
The Wyatt Quintuplets	The Dionne Quintuplets

The Dionne Quintuplets only appeared in the last ten minutes of the photoplay. They were seen squirming around in their playpen, sitting in tubs and highchairs and cooing in their beds, evoking the same response from the audience. They were fifteen months old when the movie was filmed.

The picture opened with Dr. Luke (Jean Hersholt) and Nurse Kennedy (Dorothy Peterson) battling a diptheria epidemic under adverse circumstances. It was a freezing winter day in Moosetown; the wires were down, shutting off communication with the outside world; they were running out of serum. At the last minute the doctor's nephew (Michael Whalen) arrived by plane from Montreal with the serum, thanks to a homemade radio.

Dr. Luke then traveled to Montreal to beg for a hospital. When he returned home the Constable (Slim Summerville) was on his track because it had been discovered that the doctor was practicing without a license because he was too poor to maintain the fee for it. Just as a broken-hearted Dr. Luke was boarding a boat to leave the North Woods forever because of shame and the sheriff, Asa Wyatt (John Qualen), whose six children the doctor had delivered, ran up the gangplank and begged the doctor to aid in the delivery of yet another child.

The doctor ushered quintuplets into the world for the Wyatts, achieved fame and honor, got his hospital and everyone was happy in the end.

The film was shot on Hollywood sound stages except for the sequences depicting the Quints. For this portion of the movie the director and his crew went north to Corbeil to photograph scenes under the supervision of Dr. Dafoe. The hot

Illustration 155. "Dr. Luke" (Jean Hersholt) and Dr. Dafoe in the latter's home in Callander.

lights required for filming had to have special filters placed over them to protect Dafoe's wards. All cinema equipment had to be sterilized. The actors and Director King had to have their noses and throats sprayed and they were required to don sterile gowns before they entered Dafoe Hospital to film the babies. The director and Hersholt had to adjust their behavior to that of the Quints, who could not be "directed" in the technical sense. Dafoe would only permit the girls to "work" forty-five minutes a day, and this could not interfere with their lunch or their nap.

Reviews

Frank S. Nugent in *The New York Times*: "An irresistibly appealing blend of sentiment and comedy...a mighty pleasant picture...there are splendid performances by Mr. Hersholt, Dorothy Peterson...and Frank Reicher. The minor romantic interest is carried capably."

Time: "Producer Darryl Zanuck is noted for his knack of patching stories out of histories and headlines. *The Country Doctor* is thus far the most convincing proof of his abilities in this direction. It is warm-hearted, amusing and astonishingly skillful cinema which should reward its manufacturers as handsomely as it will entertain its audiences."

Parents' Magazine: "Moving human drama with merry episodes." *Parents'* heartily recommended the film for adults, young people and children.

REUNION

Based on a story by Bruce Gould
Screenplay by Sonya Levien
Directed by Norman Taurog
A Twentieth Century-Fox Production

Roles:	Cast:
The Wyatt Quintuplets	The Dionne Quintuplets
Dr. John Luke	Jean Hersholt
Mary MacKenzie	Rochelle Hudson
Gloria Sheridan	Helen Vinson
Constable Jim Ogden	Slim Summerville
Tony Luke	Robert Kent
Nurse Katherine Kennedy	Dorothy Peterson
Asa Wyatt	John Qualen
Governor Phillip Crandall	Alan Dinehart
Charles Renard	J. Edward Bromberg
Ellie	Sara Haden
Sir Basil Crawford	Montagu Love
Dr. Richard Sheridan	Tom Moore
Rusty	George Ernest
Mrs. Martha Crandall	Katherine Alexander
Janet Fair	Esther Ralston
Sam Fisher	Julius Tannen

Illustration 156. George Chandler, Michael Whalen and June Lang in *The Country Doctor*.

Reunion ran for 80 minutes and the Dionne Quints only appeared on the screen for eight minutes. The sequel to *The Country Doctor* again concentrated on the problems of Dr. Luke (the fictional Dr. Dafoe.)

Again the action took place in Moosetown, where the president of the Chamber of Commerce persuaded Dr. Luke to hold a reunion of the 3,000 babies that he had brought into the world. During the Reunion, to which people came from all over North America, the doctor had to console a suicidal movie actress, trick a United States governor into adopting an orphan, act as matchmaker for his assistant and his nurse and save an old friend from losing his young wife. All of this was so that Twentieth Century-Fox could bring the Dionne Quintuplets, five of the guests at the Reunion, to company-owned theaters again.

The Quints were shown toddling about with two-year-old awkwardness and silence, pounding on a piano, performing acrobatics in their cribs, drinking out of their porridge bowls and sucking their thumbs. Their parents were practically discontinued from the series. The mother was not in the story; the father had only a brief role, and a fool's part at that.

Reviews

New York Times: "*Reunion* is pretty regrettable, as much for the superfluous adult presences on the screen as for the too frequent and too long absenses of the...girls. The humorous incidents...are less humorous than might have been expected.

Only the Quints themselves can be endorsed without reservation."
Time: "All this leaves the audience with renewed conviction that sequels are rarely as good as the first installment."
Parents' Magazine: "The quintuplets are more charming than ever, but the picture lacks the spontaneity of *The Country Doctor*."

FIVE OF A KIND
From a screen play by Lou Breslow and
John Patrick
Directed by Herbert I. Leeds
Produced by Sol M. Wurtzel for Twentieth
Century-Fox

Roles:	Cast:
The Wyatt Quintuplets	The Dionne Quintuplets
Dr. John Luke	Jean Hersholt
Christine Nelson	Claire Trevor
Duke Lester	Cesar Romero
Jim Ogden	Slim Summerville
Dr. Scott Williams	Henry Wilcoxon
Libby Long	Inez Courtney
Asa Wyatt	John Qualen
Mrs. Waldron	Jane Darwell
Eleanor Kingsley	Pauline Moore
Dickie	John Russell
Dr. Bruno	Andrew Tombes
Sir Basil Crawford	David Torrence
Nurse Corday	Marion Bryon
Andrew Gordon	Hamilton MacFadden
Rev. Matthew Brand	Spencer Charters
Editor Crane	Charles D. Brown

Illustration 157. Slim Summerville, Jean Hersholt and Dorothy Peterson in *The Country Doctor*.

The Reviews of *Five of a Kind* show why there were no more sequels to the continuing tale of "Dr. Luke" and the "Wyatt Quintuplets." Cuter than ever when they were four years old, the Quints did not prove to be five little Shirley Temples, much to Darryl F. Zanuck's chagrin. They certainly were not camera shy, having had one aimed at them all their lives, but their thespian ability consisted of playing with a litter of puppies, scrubbing their dolls and putting them to bed, singing half-heartedly and clumsily attemping to dance a minuet.

The plot of the film was an artificial one. It concentrated on a tangled web of rivalry and romance between two newspaper reporters and radio commentators played by Claire Trevor and Cesar Romero. The rest of the cast was once again veteran character actors in minor roles. John Qualen repeated his role as the father of the Quints, Slim Summerville was once more the Constable and Henry Wilcoxon, Jane Darwell and others tried to bring some life to the tale.

Reviews

Frank S. Nugent in *The New York Times*: "...An obviously factory-made product, with a synthetically superimposed plot...Not a trace of the humor which relieved the two earlier Dionne films. The test of a Dionne picture should not be whether the children are cute to watch, but whether it has any value apart from their presence."

Time: [The Dionne Quintuplets] "give no impression of taking their profession seriously. In the first place none of the quintuplets has bothered to learn English. In the second place, what they speak, although it sounds vaguely like French, is really some sort of squirrel talk, whose complete unintelligibility to outsiders appears to delight rather than distress the Dionnes...When they are called upon to render the simple little nursery ballad, *Frère Jacques*, [they] are so impudent as to sing it in five different keys, squealing and chuckling as they do so."

Parents' Magazine: "The Dionne Quintuplets are throughly entertaining. Rivalry between two reporters holds the film together."

So as film stars the Quints were a failure, although they earned an unprecedented salary. Twentieth Century-Fox had exclusive screen rights to their presence, but Newspaper Enterprise Association still controlled newspaper photograph rights. All stills from the films which included the Dionnes were available to NEA customers and cost magazines $50.00 each.

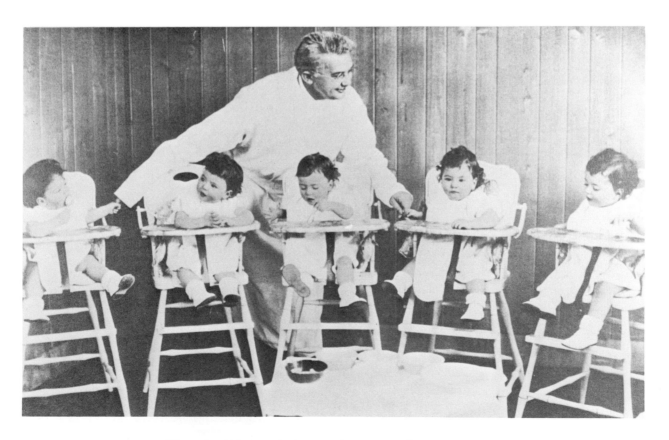

Illustration 158. Jean Hersholt and the Quints in *The Country Doctor*.

78

Illustration 159. Director Henry King showing Nurse Yvonne Leroux how the movie camera operates.

Illustration 160. Rochelle Hudson.

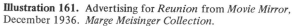

Illustration 162. Jean Hersholt was radio's "Dr. Christian" at 8:30 on Wednesday nights. In 1942 a contest was held for radio scripts with a top prize of $2,000 for the best script.

Illustration 161. Advertising for *Reunion* from *Movie Mirror*, December 1936. *Marge Meisinger Collection.*

Illustration 163. Jean Hersholt and the Dionne Quintuplets in *Five of a Kind*.

Illustration 164. The Dionne Quintuplets in *Five of a Kind*.

Illustration 165. Jean Hersholt and the Dionne Quintuplets in *Five of a Kind*.

Illustration 166. Jean Hersholt and the Dionne Quintuplets in *Five of a Kind*.

Illustration 167. The Dionne Quintuplets in *Five of a Kind*.

82

Illustration 168. Sheet music from *Five of a Kind,* published by Robbins Music Corporation in 1938. The simple tune, with lyrics by Sidney Clare, that the Quints warbled in the film, is as follows:

We're in trouble ev'ry day.
Oh! what we go through.
Won't you help us out some way?
Tell us what to do.

Five little kiddies
All mixed up.
We look like each other.

I'm "Yvonne."
Ah! Go on.
You forget
That you're "Annette."

Five little kiddies
All mixed up.
We'll find out from mother.

Ooo ooo.
Who are you?
I am "Emilie."
I'm "Cécile."
I'm "Marie."
Oh! I'm not me.

Five little kiddies
All mixed up.
It's a game we're playing.

We have fun
With everyone.
When you start
To tell us apart
First we let you,
Then we get you
All mixed up.

Lorene Anderson Collection.

VI. Paper Dolls In Sets Of Five

The Dionne Quintuplets were the best subject for play dolls ever to come along. Doll representations of famous children were always popular sellers. There had been Shirley Temple, Jane Withers, Anne Shirley, Baby Sandy Henville, Carol Ann Berry, Jackie Cooper, Jackie Coogan and other child personalities, going back to the early days of the movies; and there were many more continuing to the present day. But none of these came in fives. Five was more fun; it was also more profitable for the manufacturers.

And for parents who could not afford expensive dolls, or whose children could not wait until Christmas or any other special occasion, there were paper dolls. They were inexpensive and they had the advantage of having an extensive wardrobe and other play items to go along with them. They were a "project toy" that would keep little girls busy for hours. These were not liberated times. Dionne Quintuplet toys were only for girls.

Illustration 169. The first set of Dionne Quint paper dolls was the biggest one. The dolls, printed on heavy cardboard, as were all others, came in a large basket measuring 9-1/2 inches by 16 inches. The booklet was called *Quintuplets. The Dionne Babies. Authorized Edition of the World's Most Famous Babies*, drawn by Maud Tousey Fangel, who also did the Quints' first magazine cover. It was from the Merrill Publishing Company in 1935, no. M 3488, and included 211 pieces. Each doll measures about 6 inches high. The picture of the Quints in the basket shows, from left to right: Marie, Annette, Cécile, Emilie and Yvonne. *Marge Meisinger Collection.*

Illustration 170. Yvonne's clothes. Besides her outfits, each doll has furniture, toys, shoes and all the equipment that goes along with babies such as: playpens, dressers, bassinets, bottles, dishes, clocks and all that a baby required.

Marie

Marie

Illustration 171. Left. For "Baby Week" in April of 1936 newspapers printed paper dolls of the Quints. The doll was a photograph of each of the girls and there was a drawing of her dress to be cut out also. This is Marie from *The Commercial* of Thursday, the 23rd and she measures about 6 inches. *Marge Meisinger Collection.*

Below: Whitman, 1936, no. 1055 featured 9 inch toddlers with eight outfits each. *Marge Meisinger Collection.*

Illustration 172. Right. The Whitman Publishing Company was also a leading producer of quality paper dolls during the 1930s Their Dionne Quintuplet set from 1935 featured **actual pictures** of the Quints on the cover but the dolls, rendered by Queen Holden, were not meant to be likenesses of the Dionnes and were called *Five Paper Dolls.* Queen Holden's fame entitled her to a credit on the cover of the booklets that she designed, unlike many other artists who remained anonymous. The paperdolls are 9-1/2 inches and are **Whitman no. 998.**

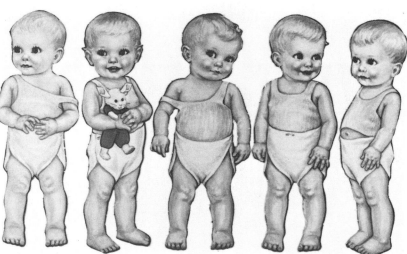

Illustration 173. Yvonne.

Illustration 174. Annette.

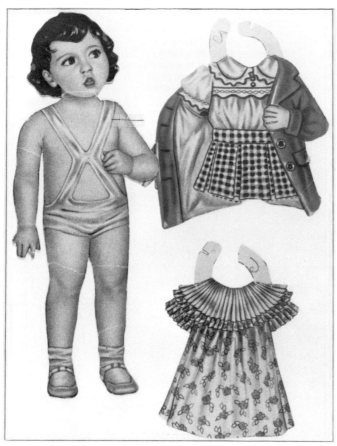

Illustration 175. Cécile.

Illustration 176. Emilie.

Illustration 177. Marie.

Illustration 178. Envelope the Palmolive Cutout booklet came in. *Marge Meisinger Collection.*

86

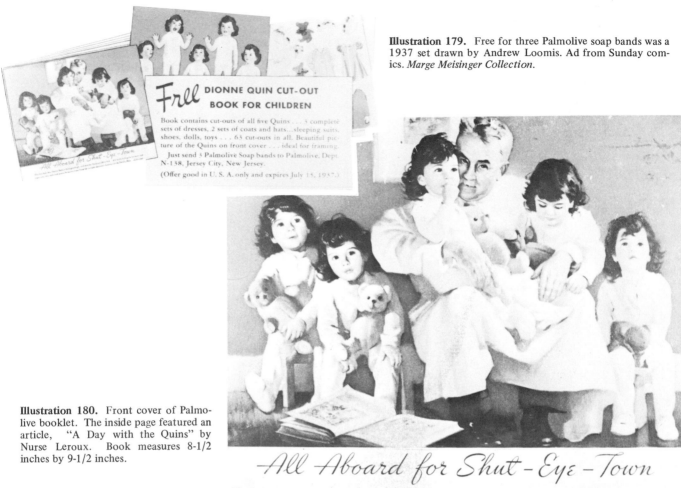

Illustration 180. Front cover of Palmolive booklet. The inside page featured an article, "A Day with the Quins" by Nurse Leroux. Book measures 8-1/2 inches by 9-1/2 inches.

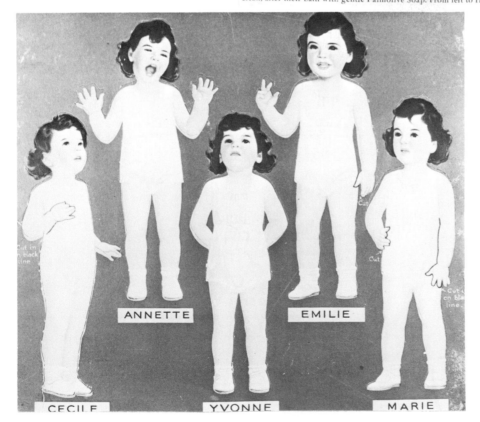

Illustration 181. Back cover. The dolls average 5-3/4 inches high.

Illustrations 182 & 183. Two of the four pages of cutouts.

Illustration 184. *Five Dionne Quintuplets Cutout Doll Book,* from Dell Publishing Company in 1937, featured rather sketchily drawn 9 inch dolls depicting the Dionne Quintuplets when they were about three-years-old. *Lorene Anderson Collection.*

Illustration 185. In 1940 Merrill offered a set of five booklets of paper dolls, no. 3500 A to E. Each booklet measured 9-1/2 inches by 10-1/2 inches; the dolls are about 8-1/2 inches high. *Marge Meisinger Collection.*

Illustration 186. Back of Marie booklet. (All the backs are identical.)

Illustrations 187 & 188. Two of the four pages of Marie's clothes and clothing for her doll.

Illustration 189. Annette. *Lorene Anderson Collection.*

Illustration 190. Emilie. *Lorene Anderson Collection.*

Illustration 192. Cécile from a booklet that has been cut out. *Lorene Anderson Collection.*

Illustration 191. Above. Yvonne. *Lorene Anderson Collection.*

Illustration 193. No. 3488, Merrill, 1940. *Mary Stuecher Collection.*

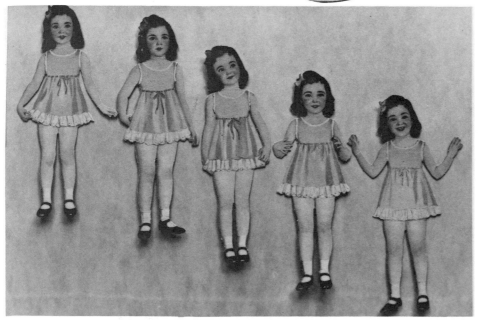

Illustration 194. A thoughtful mother and a daughter who respected her playthings insured the survival of this cut set of paper dolls over the years. The dolls measure 8 inches and they are, left to right, Yvonne, Annette, Cécile, Emilie and Marie. *Mary Stuecher Collection.*

Illustration 195. Each doll in this set had eight changes, including the fairy tale costumes from the newspaper "plays" featuring the Quints.

Illustration 196. The booklet included heavy cardboard toys for each doll, like the baby buggy filled with quint dolls shown here.

Illustration 197. A "knock-off" is an item similar to a popular one that can cash in on its success without the problem of royalties. The "Five Cut-Out Dolly Sisters" is an example of a knock-off on Dionne paper dolls. This booklet from the Whitman Publishing Company in 1939 looks familiar. The doll of Patsy measures 9-3/4 inches. The other Dolly Sisters were Bunny, Margie, Dotty and Peggy; and of course they all appeared to be the same ages!

Illustration 198. Quintuplets were popular all over again in 1963. Quintuplet boys were born on September 7 to Sr. and Sra. Efren Lubin Prieto in Maracaibo, Venezuela and four girls and a boy were born on September 14 to Mr. and Mrs. Andrew Fischer of Aberdeen, South Dakota. Up to that time these were the only sets born in the Western Hemisphere besides the Dionnes and the Diligentis. *Good Housekeeping* gained exclusive rights to the American set and there was some publicity but they never captured the public imagination as had the Dionnes. Some quintuplet items were marketed for a while. The Saalfield Publishing Co. offered paper dolls in 1964, no. 1352, which sold for 29 cents. *Marge Meisinger Collection.*

Illustration 199. Back of the Saalfield booklet showing the five dolls.

Illustration 200. The Western Publishing Company, Inc. came out with a small booklet, measuring 8-1/4 inches by 11 inches in 1964 and 1967.

Illustration 201. Back of the Western booklet showing the three girls and two boys. The quintuplet dolls measure about 4 inches.

94

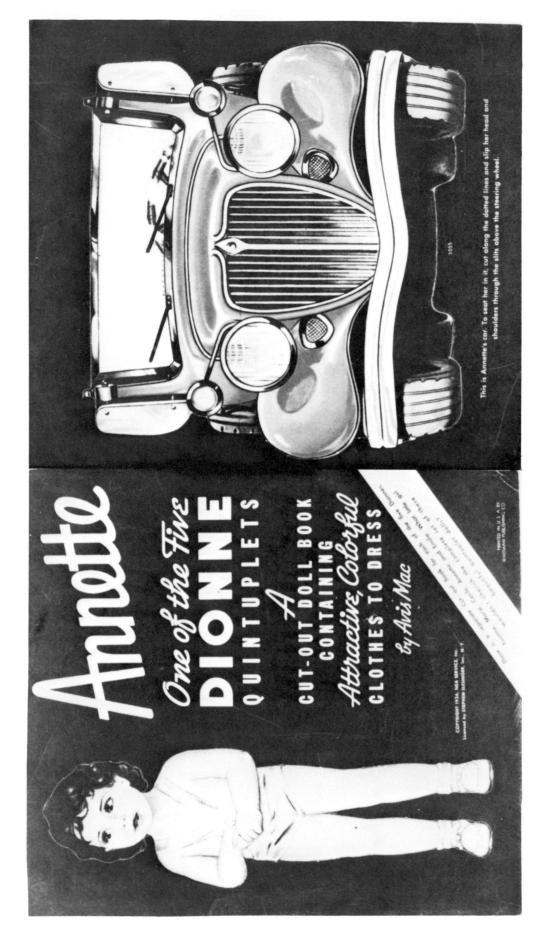

This is Annette's car. To seat her in it, cut along the dotted lines and slip her head and shoulders through the slits above the steering wheel.

1055

Annette

One of the Five

DIONNE

QUINTUPLETS

A

CUT-OUT DOLL BOOK
CONTAINING

Attractive, Colorful

CLOTHES TO DRESS

by Avis Mac

COPYRIGHT 1936, NEA SERVICE, Inc.
Licensed by STEPHEN SLESINGER, Inc., N. Y.

Illustration 202. Cover of *One of the Five Dionne Quintuplets* by Avis Mac, the Whitman set of 1936 that is similar to the later "knock-off" booklets. All of the back covers of the set featured a similar car in which to place each Quint.

Illustration 203. A wooden ferris wheel was marketed by Alexander so that the 7 inch Quint baby dolls could be given a ride! The overall size is approximately 19 inches and the wheel is about 15 inches in diameter. It is made of wood, the wheel painted yellow and blue and the base a pale green, and at one time had a handle protruding from the center to turn it. The picture of the Dionnes on the front and the names at each seat are decals in color. *Jimmy and Fay Rodolfos Collection.*

96

Illustration 204. Cover of *Wards 1935 Christmas Catalog* showing the Dionne Quintuplet dolls in color. There were four different sizes of dolls offered and all of them had molded straight hair. (The sizes listed do not correspond to the correct measurements, a fault with most catalog descriptions of dolls.) All of the dolls were babies with curved legs. They all wore white organdy dresses, bonnets and slips and all had a bib with the name of the Quint embroidered on it in the color assigned by Madame Alexander. Yvonne wore pink, Annette yellow, Cécile green, Emilie lavender and Marie blue. (The colors the real Quints wore for identification purposes were Yvonne pink, Annette red, Cécile green, Emilie white and Marie blue.) The two smaller sizes wore a diaper and booties; the next to smallest size had no bonnet; the two larger sizes had cloth bodies, wore sox and moccasins and rubber panties. All the dolls except the smallest size, which had painted eyes, had brown sleep eyes and lashes. The four sizes sold for 79 cents, $1.69, $2.69 and $4.39. The three larger sizes could also be ordered wearing pink corduroy coats and bonnets selling for $2.69, $4.39 and $5.79. The smallest size also came in a wooden enameled bed and sold for $4.39 for the complete set, including all five Quint dolls.

VII. Dolls Of Real Dolls

The only "genuine" Dionne Quintuplet dolls were those manufactured by the Alexander Doll Company of New York City from 1935 to 1939. This company concluded a secret agreement with the guardians of the Quints in which they received exclusive rights to manufacture dolls bearing the Dionne name. Almost every known doll company during the same period released dolls which resembled the famous Quint babies and stores obligingly displayed them in groups of fives. Japanese and German manufacturers of dolls of an inferior quality (but not always) packaged small sets in boxes of five, sometimes with a nurse and often called them "Five Sisters," "Quintuplets," or "Quinties"; but these were never advertised as Dionnes, although they sold just as well for it was obvious to purchasers who they were.

Beatrice Alexander Behrman, known as Madame Alexander in the doll world, has been producing quality dolls since she founded her company in 1923. She is still producing dolls today. Madame Alexander dolls, including versions in current production are the most popular collectible dolls ever made in the United States. The parents of Madame Alexander, after having emigrated to America from Russia, founded the first doll repair hospital in New York City in 1895. Mrs. Behrman was born into doll making. She had the vision to create only first-class dolls and concentrated on doll characters that had already achieved popularity in other mediums.

The first Madame Alexander commercial doll was Alice in Wonderland from the Lewis Carroll classic. This doll has remained in the line through the years and has appeared in every type of manufacturing material used by doll makers since her inception. Alice was made in cloth, felt, molded composition, hard plastic, and presently in vinyl. Current Alexander dolls are the ever-popular baby doll, small dolls of storybook characters and beautiful girl and lady dolls. Movie star and personality dolls were the best sellers during the "Golden Age" of modern dolls. There were different versions of Jane Withers and Sonja Henie, Princess Elizabeth and Margaret O'Brien, and the most popular of all—the Dionne Quintuplets.

The Dionne Quintuplet dolls first came out in time for Christmas of 1935. They were designed by Bernard Lipfert, who learned his craft in pre-War Germany, and who created all of the popular dolls of the period, including Shirley Temple, the most prodigious doll ever produced in America. By 1936 the three best-selling dolls in the country were the creations of this one man, who completely monopolized American doll designing after Germany lost the market because of two World Wars. Behind

Shirley Temple from Ideal Novelty and Toy Company there was EffanBee's Dy-Dee Baby and Madame Alexander's Dionnes were in third place.

Alexander dolls have always been famous for the attention given to details in the costuming and for the high-quality fabrics and accessories used. For the materials employed in the construction of the doll itself superior standards were always maintained. After nearly a half century Madame Alexander composition dolls are less crazed and cracked and the eyes have not become as crystalized as are other better dolls of the 1920s, 30s, and 40s. Composition, made from resin, wood flour, starch and water, is the most susceptible to the passing of time of any material from which play dolls were ever rendered. Alexander dolls were always more expensive than dolls from other companies. And they were always worth more.

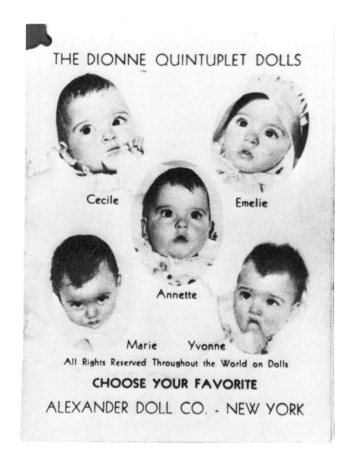

Illustration 205. Booklet that was attached to each doll or to each set of dolls. The Alexander Doll Company spelled Emilie's name "Emelie" in advertising and on the name pins at first.

Madame Alexander was no *schlump* when it came to advertising her dolls. She appealed to little girls, who could do the "selling" for her. A pamphlet that came with Dionne Quintuplet dolls in 1935 told the little ones to "Choose Your Favorite ...Complete your collection of these darling babies by being a good girl. Ma may get you one, then Pa another. Then there are Aunty Jane and Uncle Bill —they will want to please you, too, and help get this happy family." Only the smaller, less expensive sets of Quints were sold together. The larger dolls were sold separately and no little girl ever planned to settle for one or two. Then the advertising for Quintuplet dolls enticed her more: "Ask to see their nurse and doctor dolls." Little girls longed for the complete set of Quint dolls; relatives wondered how they would fill this real need; and Alexander Doll Company sales soared.

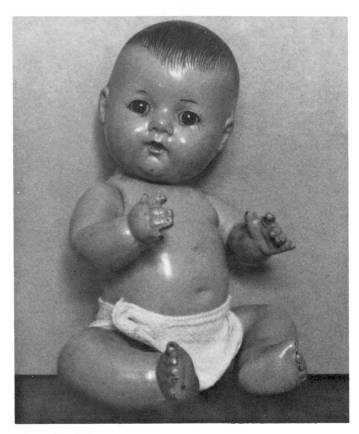

Illustration 207. 10 inch, all composition with movable head, arms and legs. Marked on head: "Dionne"/Alexander. Marked on back: Madame/Alexander. Brown sleep eyes and lashes. *Connie Chase Collection.*

Illustration 206. 7 inch, all composition with movable head, arms and legs. Marked on head: Dionne/Alexander. Marked on back: Alexander. This is Marie from the set in the bed and she wears her original diaper, undershirt and bib, which was all this set came with. The painted brown eyes are glancing to the doll's right.

Illustration 208. Close-up of 10 inch size baby. *Lois Barrett Collection.*

The Madame Alexander Dionne Quintuplet Dolls [1]

Babies - in inches

Inches	Description	Markings
7	All composition straight hair painted eyes	Head: Dionne/Alexander Back: Alexander
7	All composition curly hair painted eyes	Head and Back: Alexander
10	All composition straight hair closed mouth	Head: "Dionne"/Alexander Back: Madame/Alexander
11-1/2	Cloth body curly hair open mouth	Head: Alexander
16-1/2	Cloth body straight hair closed mouth	Head: "Dionne"/Alexander
17-1/2	Cloth body curly hair closed mouth	Head: Alexander
23	Cloth body straight hair open mouth	Head: "Dionne"/Alexander

Toddlers - in inches

Inches	Description	Markings
7-1/2	All composition Mohair wig over straight hair painted eyes	Head: Dionne/Alexander Back: Alexander
7-1/2	All composition curly hair painted eyes	Head and Back: Alexander
11-1/2	All composition Mohair wig over straight hair closed mouth	Head: "Dionne"/Alexander Back: Madame/Alexander
11-1/2	All composition curly hair closed mouth	Head: Alexander
11-1/2	All composition curly hair open mouth	Head and Back: Alexander
11-1/2	All composition curly hair open mouth	Head: Alexander Back: Madame/Alexander

---

[1]The author concedes that there may be other variations in existence.

11-1/2	All composition (can be 11-1/4) chubby legs curly hair open mouth	Head: Alexander Back: Madame/Alexander
11-1/2	All composition human hair wig over plain head closed mouth	Head: "Dionne"/Alexander Back: Madame/Alexander
11-1/2	All composition human hair wig over plain head open mouth	Head: "Dionne"/Alexander Back: Alexander
14-1/2	All composition curly hair closed mouth	Head and Back: Alexander
14-1/2	All composition human hair wig over plain head open mouth	Back: Alexander
17	All composition curly hair closed mouth	Head and Back: Alexander
17	All composition human hair wig over plain head closed mouth	Back: Alexander
17	All composition human hair wig over plain head open mouth	Back: Alexander
19-1/2	All composition human hair wig over molded straight hair closed mouth	Head and Back: Alexander
19-1/2	All composition human hair wig over plain head open mouth	Back: Alexander

Girls in inches

Inches	Description	Markings
13-1/2	Cloth body human hair wig over plain head closed mouth	Head: "Dionne"/Alexander
17	Cloth body human hair wig over plain head open mouth	*no markings on doll*

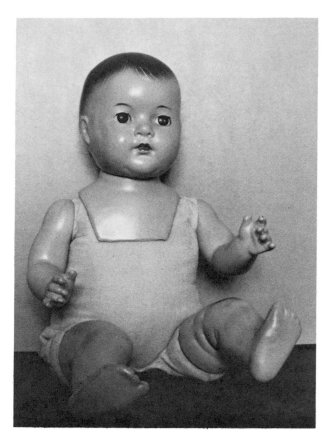

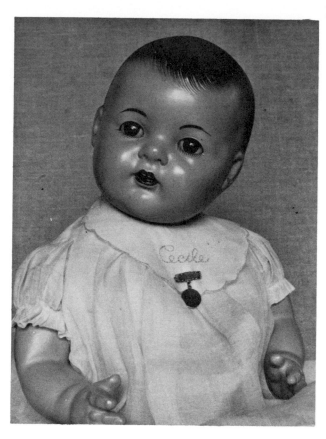

Illustration 209. 16-1/2 inch composition swivel head on shoulder-plate, composition arms and legs. The soft cloth body has a cry voice. Marked on head: "Dionne"/Alexander. Brown sleep eyes and lashes. *Connie Chase Collection.*

Illustration 210. Close-up of Barbara DeVault's Cécile. The gold pin is engraved with her name; the reverse reads: Madame Alexander. If the pin is original to this doll it would date it after 1936, as the Ward's catalog for 1935 does not mention pins.

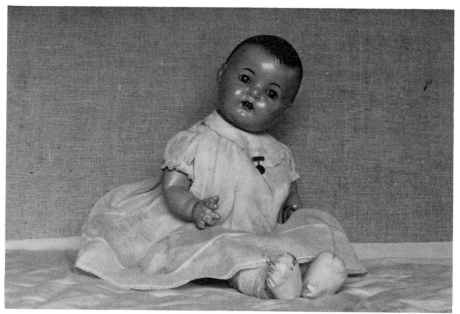

Illustration 211. 23 inch Cécile. The construction and the markings are the same as the 16-1/2 inch size, the only difference being an open mouth with a tongue and two upper teeth. The original dress carries a label reading: Dionne Quintuplets/Madame Alexander/Reg. N.Y. *Barbara DeVault Collection.*

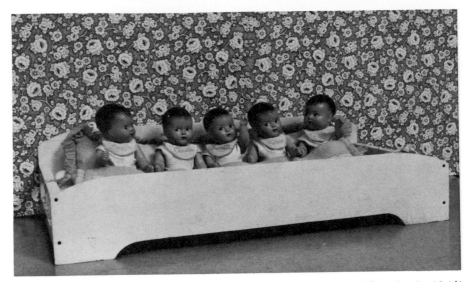

Illustration 212. 7 inch Quints in wooden bed. The bed measures 19-7/8 inches by 10-1/4 inches. The headboard is 5 inches high; the footboard is 3-3/4 inches high. The set includes a pink cotton covered mattress, two pink silk bound cotton blankets and a pink dotted swiss pillow with a ruffle around the edges and rosettes at each corner. This outfit looks just as it did in 1935, as it was never played with.

Illustration 213. Rochelle Hudson, star of the second Dionne Quintuplet film *Reunion*, holding a set of Quint dolls like those offered by Sears for Christmas of 1936.

FAMOUS DIONNE QUINTUPLET DOLLS
THE ADORABLE BABIES HAVE GROWN UP
© NEA SERVICE INC.

"These Dionne Quintuplet Dolls are the only authorized doll replicas of the famous Dionne Quintuplets by special permission of their guardians."
(SIGNED) **David A. Croll**
MINISTER OF PUBLIC WELFARE, PROVINCE OF ONTARIO, CANADA

ANNETTE   EMILIE   CECILE   YVONNE   MARIE

NAME PIN WITH EACH DOLL

JUST AS THEY LOOK TODAY . . . And They Can Stand Up, Too

Look at them—"Darlings, every one!"—reproduced in miniature by one of America's greatest sculptors of dolls—so true to life, you'd swear they were live, breathing, laughing, adorable little girls. Into these little, straight leg dolls the artist has by some miracle of genius transmitted the true expressions, the wide-open charm of their famous big dark, understanding eyes, and the full beauty of their adorable curly dark brown hair—yes—even the humanly soft skin coloring of their roly-poly baby faces and the true shape of each tiny head.

They are full composition, with inside jointed, turning tilting head, arms and legs. Daintily dressed in excellent quality lacy organdy dress and lacy bonnet to match, tied with ribbon. Pretty organdy undies, rayon socks and snap buckle imitation leather shoes.

The world can no more resist loving these new dolls than could they help taking the actual "Quints" to their hearts. They are all here, Yvonne, Marie, Cecile, Emilie, Annette.

Name of each Dionne Quintuplet Doll is stamped on gold plated pin included with each. Order by Name.

NEW BEAUTIES With Real Dark Brown RINGLET HAIR	IRRESISTIBLE Babies In Dark Brown PAINTED HAIR
$2.25 EACH 11½ In.	**$1.85 EACH** 11½ In.
The most popular kind. Big appealing, glass-like eyes with real long lashes; dainty rosebud mouth.	Attractively priced. Big, open, wistful, glass-like eyes with real long lashes.

11½ IN. TALL 49 V 3279 Shpg. wt., 2 lbs.	14½ IN. TALL 49 V 3280 Shpg. wt., 2 lbs. 8 oz.
$2.25	**$3.79**

11½ INCHES TALL
49 V 3284
Shipping weight, 1 lb. 6 oz. **$1.85**

Same as above but with painted eyes and painted lashes. Shipping weight, 8 ounces.
49 V 3278 ... 7½ In. Tall. **$1.15**

Same as above but with painted eyes, lashes and mouth. Shpg. wt., 8 oz.
49 V 3283 7½ In. Tall **89c**

PAINTED HAIR

THE FIVE FAMOUS "DIONNE QUINTS"
MARIE—YVONNE—CECILE—EMILIE—ANNETTE
IN 20-INCH ENAMELED WOOD BED

All five of the "Famous Dionne Quints" reproduced into lovely dolls. They look so much alike that you could not tell them apart if they did not wear their names on the gold plated pin fastened to each **dainty little lace trimmed romper.** Silk ribbon tied lace trimmed bonnet to match. Five little bundles of joy. 7½ in. full inside jointed composition dolls. Painted eyes, brown painted hair nestled on soft cotton stuffed pillow covered with pretty dotted material. Soft cotton stuffed mattress. Cover trimmed with picot edged organdy and over all a soft baby blanket and just the right size. 20-in. white enameled wood bed with name of each Dionne Quint Doll lettered on foot. Shipping weight, 3 pounds.

49 V 3501   5 Dolls, Bed and Outfit   **$4.49**   **$4.49 Complete**

↑ SEARS-ROEBUCK 3

Illustration 214. Page from Sears Christmas catalog of 1936. David A. Croll, a guardian of the Quints and Ontario's Minister of Public Welfare, endorsed the dolls: "These Dionne Quintuplet Dolls are the only authorized doll replicas of the famous Dionne Quintuplets by special permission of their guardians." The ad featured three sizes of two-year-old toddlers in all-composition, fully-jointed with "dark, curly brown hair" (probably mohair) and "dainty rosebud mouths." All the dolls wore organdy dresses, bonnets and undies and had imitation leather shoes. Two sizes of babies were featured, in all composition, with dark brown painted hair. A different set of babies was again sold as a complete outfit in the wooden bed.

Illustration 215A. 11-1/2 inch all-composition, fully-jointed toddler with brown sleep eyes, lashes and the closed mouth. Marked on head: "Dionne"/Alexander. Marked on back: Madame/Alexander. The head is the same as that of the 10 inch baby of 1935 but has a brown mohair wig glued over the molded hair. She has chubby legs that are rather bent at the knees. The pale blue organdy dress and bonnet appear to be original although there is no evidence of labels.

Illustration 215B. Detailed close-up of picture Illustration 215A.

Illustration 216. 7-1/2 inch all-composition, fully-jointed toddler with brown painted eyes. Marked on head: Dionne/Alexander. Marked on back: Alexander. This is also the same doll mold as the baby of 1935 with a wig over the molded hair and straight instead of curved legs. The original dress and underpants combination are lavender with a tag reading: Genuine/Dionne Quintuplet Dolls/All rights reserved/Madame Alexander–N. Y. She is wearing her "Emelie" pin.

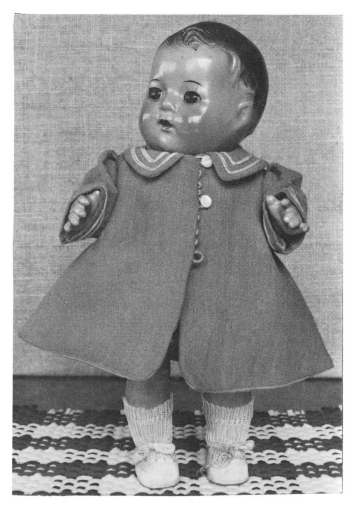

Illustration 217. 11-1/2 inch all-composition, fully-jointed toddler with brown sleep eyes and painted curly hair. Marked on head: Alexander. No markings on body. The yellow wool coat, though not original to this doll, carries the same Alexander label as the other Quintuplet doll clothes of 1936.

Illustration 218. 11-3/4 inch all-composition, fully-jointed toddler like Illustration 217, although the paint finish is more matte and the body is also marked: Alexander. The doll is somewhat cracked and crazed (which also helps to make the size difference); but she wears a blue outfit, including shoes, shown in the 1936 Sears ad. The dress label was removed sometime in the past.

Illustration 219. 11-1/2 inch toddlers in three different original outfits with the labels reading like the other ones of 1936. The shoes and sox are not original. The colors are (left to right) pink, lavender and yellow for identification of which doll it represents. The two dolls on either end are marked: Alexander on the head and back. The center doll is marked: Alexander on the head; Madame/Alexander on the body. *Connie Chase Collection*.

Illustration 220. 7-1/2 inch all-composition, fully-jointed toddlers with brown painted eyes and brown painted molded curly hair. Marked on head and back: Alexander. The organdy outfits of pink and green are all original. (The name pins do not coincide with the colors of the dresses; therefore they are not original to the dolls.) *Connie Chase Collection.*

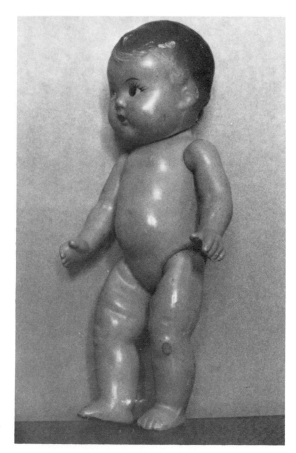

Illustration 221. 7-1/2 inch toddler showing the body construction. *Connie Chase Collection.*

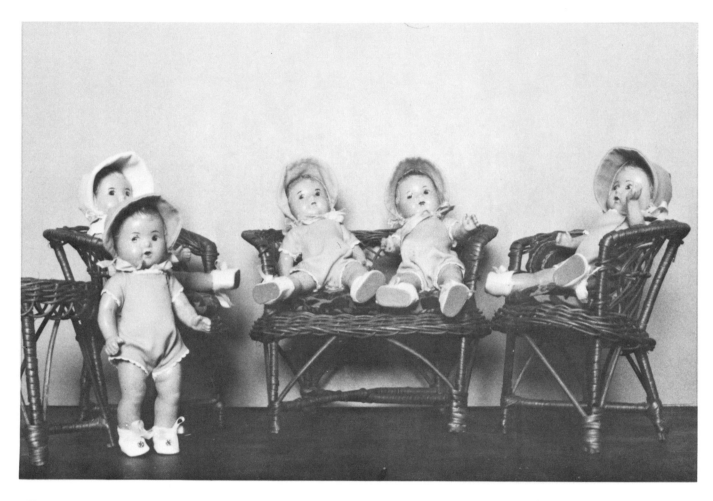

Illustration 222. 7-1/2 inch toddlers with the curly painted hair. They are wearing all-original sunsuits and bonnets of corduroy. *Connie Chase Collection.*

Illustration 223. 7 inch all-composition, fully-jointed babies with painted curly hair and painted eyes. Marked on heads and bodies: Alexander. The corduroy suits are labeled; the pins are original. The body construction is the same as that of the straight-hair babies of 1935, with the curved legs. *Lois Barrett Collection.*

Illustration 224. 7 inch curly haired baby from Lois Barrett's set, which she received for Christmas as a child.

110

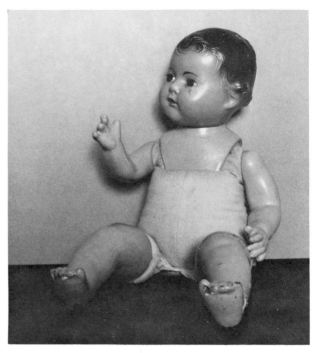

Illustration 225. Alexander Doll Co. ad from *Modern Screen*, April 1937. The dolls were again shown as babies. Madame Alexander advertising promised that the Quints would be presented as they were at the time; but babies and toddlers were the most popular dolls, so they were continued.

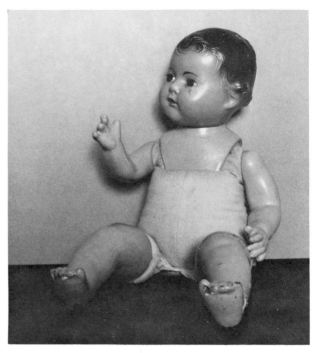

Illustration 226. 17-1/2 inch cloth-body baby with molded curly hair, closed mouth, brown sleep eyes and lashes. Marked on head: Alexander. *Connie Chase Collection.*

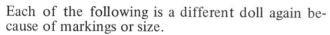

Each of the following is a different doll again because of markings or size.

Illustration 227. 14-1/2 inch all-composition toddler with molded curly hair, closed mouth, brown sleep eyes and lashes. Marked on head and body: Alexander. The doll is dressed all original as Marie. The dress label reads: Dionne Quintuplets/Madame Alexander/New York. This doll with deeper hair modeling represents an older toddler than the ones produced in 1936. *Connie Chase Collection.*

Illustration 228. The same toddler in the 17 inch size. Clothing not original. *Barbara DeVault Collection.*

Illustration 229A. 11-1/2 inch toddlers, all composition with closed mouth, brown sleep eyes and lashes. Human hair wig over plain head. Marked on head: "Dionne"/Alexander. Marked on back: Madame/Alexander. The clothing is not original. *Connie Chase Collection.*

Illustration 229B. 11-1/2 inch toddlers, all composition with open mouth, four teeth, brown sleep eyes and lashes. Human hair wig over plain head. Marked on head: "Dionne"/Alexander. Marked on back: Alexander. Outfits not original. *Connie Chase Collection.*

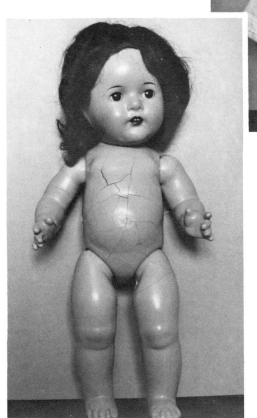

Illustration 230. 14-1/2 inch toddler. All composition with open mouth, four teeth, brown sleep eyes and lashes. Human hair wig over plain head. Marked only on back: Alexander. Note proportionately chubbier legs than on the 11-1/2 inch toddlers of the same type. *Connie Chase Collection.*

Illustration 231. 11-1/4 inch toddlers with chubby legs. All composition with open mouth, four teeth, brown sleep eyes and lashes, painted curly hair. Marked on heads: Alexander. Marked on back: Madame/Alexander. These flowered print dresses are the most attractive of all the costumes designed for the Quint dolls by Madame Alexander. Marie, at left, with blue dominating in her outfit wears her name on a medal on a chain; Cécile, in the center, in green, wears the pin; Annette, on the right, wears the pin and yellow dominates in her dress. These dolls are all original with the dress tag reading: Genuine/Dionne Quintuplet Dolls/All Rights Reserved/Madame Alexander—N.Y. *Connie Chase Collection.*

Illustration 232. Above. Close-up of Connie Chase's Cécile.

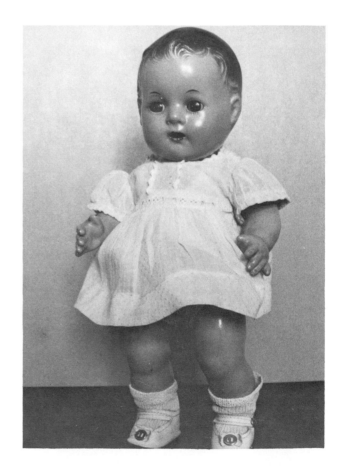

Illustration 233. Right. 11-1/2 inch all-original toddler. The sizes of dolls vary, depending on the component parts used; but this doll is marked in the same way as the set in the print dresses. In the January and April 1939 *Parents' Magazine,* a Dionne Quintuplet doll wearing this dress and also a matching bonnet was offered free for three one-year subscriptions or three renewals, not counting "gift subscriptions" or "your own subscription." In 1937 *Parents'* had offered a Shirley Temple doll for two subscriptions and later in 1939 the prize was a Jane Withers doll and in 1940 it was McGuffey Ana, both from Madame Alexander. *Connie Chase.*

Illustration 234. 17 inch all-original toddlers with labeled dresses. Fully jointed composition, closed mouth, brown sleep eyes and lashes. The human hair wigs, as on all larger toddlers, are glued over a plain head. The name tags are on a chain. Marked on back: Alexander. *Connie Chase Collection.*

Illustration 235. Close-up of Yvonne. *Connie Chase Collection.*

Illustration 236. 17 inch all-original Yvonne toddler with labeled dotted swiss dress. Fully jointed, open mouth, four teeth, brown sleep eyes, lashes, human hair wig. Only the body is marked: Alexander. *Lois Barrett Collection.*

Illustration 237. 17 inch all-original toddlers of the same type. This is an exceptional set and no doubt the only one like it in existence. The dolls are wearing labeled corduroy playsuits under their wool coats, leggings and hats. Each outfit is of the proper color and each doll wears her name pin. The coats are also tagged with the usual Madame Alexander label of the later Quint dolls. *Donna Stanley Collection.*

Illustration 238. Close-up of Lois Barrett's Yvonne.

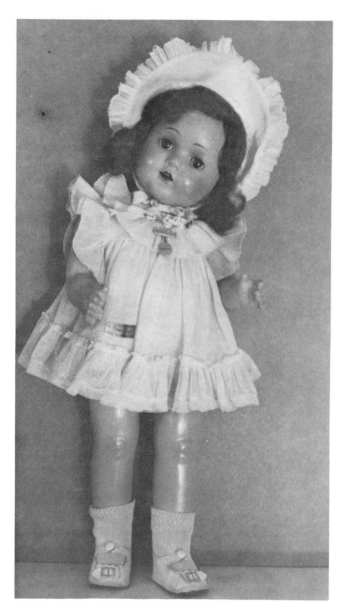

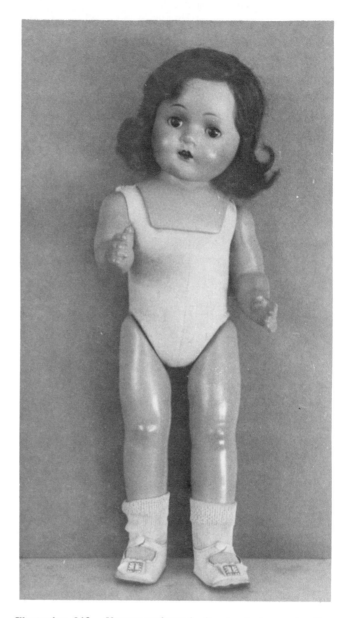

Illustration 239. 17 inch like-new Yvonne child. Composition swivel head on shoulder plate, full arms and legs. Tightly stuffed cloth body. Human hair wig, brown sleep eyes, lashes, open mouth with four teeth. The legs are thinner and straighter than on the toddler dolls. This doll is not marked at all; her pin and the tag on her dress carry the Madame Alexander markings. The gold paper label on the front of the dress refers to the wig and reads: Human Hair.

Illustration 240. Yvonne undressed, showing body construction.

Illustration 241. Close-up of Yvonne.

LOT. No

Marie

Cecile

MADAME ALEXANDER
New York, N. Y.

Annette

Yvonne

Emilie

Illustration 242. The original Madame Alexander box in which Yvonne was packaged.

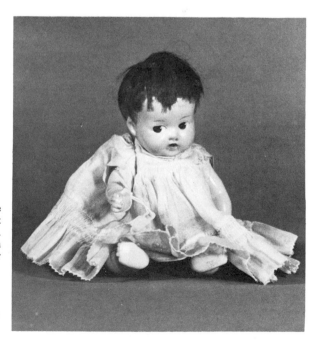

Illustration 243. This doll resembles the 7 inch Dionne Quintuplet babies and is also from Madame Alexander but would date from an earlier period because of the markings. She is 7 inches and is constructed like the Quint dolls in fully-jointed composition, but has a mohair wig glued on her head. The head is marked:

A D Co

and the body is marked:

ALEXANDER

She could possibly be a prototype for the modeling of the Dionne Quintuplet dolls. *Jimmy and Fay Rodolfos.*

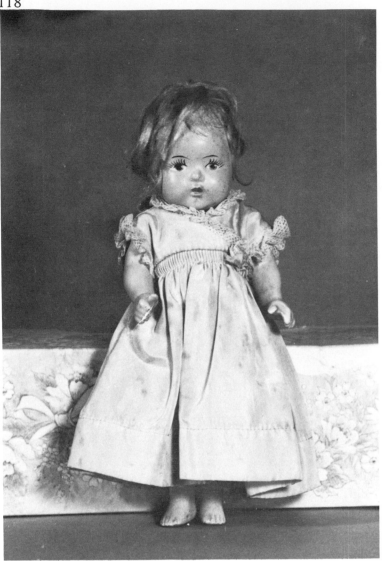

Illustration 244. Doll makers did not waste spare parts in assembling dolls. This is Princess Elizabeth in her original, tagged dress from Madame Alexander. The head is from the regular Dionne Quintuplet mold and is marked:

DIONNE

ALEXANDER

The blond mohair wig is glued over the unpainted, straighthair head. The eyes are painted blue. The back is marked:

ALEXANDER

and is the same torso used for the Quint dolls. The legs are thinner than those found on a Dionne toddler and are like the ones on the small Wendy Anns. This doll would probably date from the very late 1930s. *Jimmy and Fay Rodolfos.*

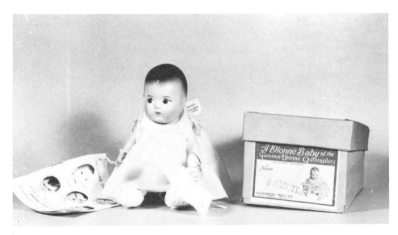

Illustration 245. A 7 inch Cécile, carrying the Dionne/Alexander marking, with her original box. The doll looks like she was manufactured yesterday and she still retains the original matte finish of the composition as she was not handled in the last 40 years. The picture shows the doll exactly as she would have been presented for sale in the late 1930s.

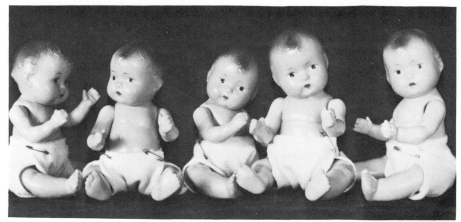

Illustration 246. The Dionne Quintuplet dolls were *not* the only quintuplet dolls! Many other dolls sold in sets of five once they were in the store because they cost less or the Madame Alexander dolls were not available. These "Quints" are 6-1/2 inches and were purchased as a set for a Christmas gift in the late 1930s. Marked on head: EffanBee. Marked on back: EffanBee/Baby Tinyette. Fully-jointed composition with brown painted hair and blue painted eyes. The diapers are original.

Illustration 247. The Arranbee Doll Company had their own version of the Dionne Quintuplet doll, copying Madame Alexander's design in the same general size. Wearing an all-original outfit, this 7-1/2 inch baby has red painted hair, blue painted eyes and is constructed like the composition Quints dolls, which dates her from the same period. She is marked on the back:
R & B
DOLL CO.
Jimmy and Fay Rodolfos

Illustration 248. 7 inch unmarked babies. They are fully-jointed composition with the same curved legs as the small Madame Alexander Quints and the EffanBee Tinyettes. They are not as well finished as the better dolls; the brown hair and the brown eyes are not as neatly painted. These dolls are selling as "Unmarked Dionne Quintuplets" at ridiculous prices today, yet they were never marketed as Dionnes, which would have violated the Alexander authorization. Some dolls using this same mold are marked on the head: Superior. They came with both brown and blue eyes. Dolls are redressed.

Illustration 249. Close-up of unmarked Quint type. Original diaper.

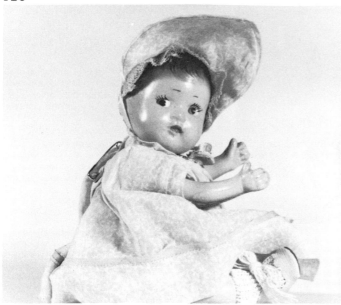

Illustration 250. 7 inch unmarked of the same modeling in an all-original outfit. The brown eyes on this doll are painted more nearly like those of the Madame Alexander dolls, including the same type of painted lashes.

Illustration 251. A black version of the 7 inch unmarked Dionne Quint type doll with bent baby legs. She is fully-jointed composition and has painted features and painted hair with three tufts of yarn hair attached from the inside through holes in the head. *Jimmy and Fay Rodolfos.*

Illustration 252. 16 inch unmarked cloth-body baby. Composition flange-type head, arms, lower legs. Black painted hair, brown tin sleep eyes, open mouth with two teeth. She wears her original blue organdy dress and bonnet. Mary Stuecher received this doll for Christmas in 1936 and it was understood at the time that this was a "Dionne Quintuplet." *Mary Stuecher Collection.*

Illustration 253. Another unmarked 7 inch Quint type with black hair and blue eyes, also more finely painted.

Illustration 254. 14 inch unmarked toddler using the same construction as the Alexander Quint toddlers. Fully-jointed composition, brown painted hair, blue tin sleep eyes, lashes, open mouth with two teeth. This doll is all original and in like-new condition although she is a cheaply made doll of the early 1940s. These dolls sold in the 5 & 10's for about a dollar. The mold marks are not sanded and finished as well as the better dolls and the clothing is cotton of a simple design.

Illustration 255. The best and the worst imitations used to come from Japan. This 6-1/2 inch bent-limb baby is made of a durable papier-mâché and is fully jointed. The detailing in the modeling is better than that of the Alexander dolls. The molded hair is brown; the painted eyes are blue. This excellent quality doll from the late 1930s was part of a set of five and is marked on the back: JAPAN.

Illustration 256. 5-1/8 inch all-bisque, with jointed arms and legs. Marked: ③/Made in Japan. The hair and the eyes are painted in the same manner as the Madame Alexander babies. The clothing appears to be original. *Connie Chase Collection.*

Illustration 257. 2-5/8 inch all-bisque with jointed arms. Marked: Made in/ Occupied/Japan. The dress is original. The doll came in a box of five identical dolls with different colored dresses and was purchased new after World War II. *Childhood toy of Bette Ann Axe.*

Illustration 258. 3-7/8 inch all-bisque dolls with movable arms in the original box. The dolls have brightly painted gold and silver hair; the facial features are poorly sketched. The clothing is silk floss wound around the upper torso and silk glued-on skirts. The dolls and the skirts are marked: Made in Japan. There were many similar sets of five dolls of this type from Japan in the late 1930s to capitalize on the rage for the Quints. They sold for about 25 cents in the dime stores; today that figure could be translated into dollars.

Illustration 259. 1-1/4 inch bisque figurine from Japan. Tea cup for size relation.

Illustration 260. Some sets of the 7 inch Madame Alexander babies were sold in a wooden wagon for five called the "Quint-O-Bile." There was also a long highchair that held all five babies in a row, a Merry-Go-'Round and other wooden accessories. In 1936 Alexander sold a "Dionne Quintuplet's Home," a large cardboard room containing the five 7 inch babies and a nurse doll. There was wooden furniture for the five dolls: a bed; a scooter; a highchair; a low chair; a playpen. The last two itmes are pictured here. *Connie Chase Collection.*

Illustration 261. In 1964 The Alexander Doll Company introduced a new set of quintuplet dolls. In order not to violate the *Good Housekeeping* "exclusive rights," they were not advertised as the Fischer Quints, but four of the dolls had a pink baby bottle and one had a blue one. The dolls are 7 inches. The head is hard plastic and the jointed body is vinyl. All the dolls had blue sleep eyes with molded plastic lashes and open mouths for the bottles. The dolls were not marked and came in unlabeled undershirts and diapers. The same doll was used for Alexander's Little Genius in tagged clothing. *Marge Meisinger Collection.*

Illustration 262. 14-1/2 inch all-original "Dr. Dafoe." This all-composition doll was advertised by Alexander as a "doctor doll for the Quints" but was not billed as Dafoe. The body is fully jointed and has a bent right arm, like Alexander's "Little Betty." Painted blue eyes, dimple in chin, gray wig. The doll is not marked but the original white cotton outfit is a one-piece pants and shirt with a doctor's smock over top, labeled. Madame/Alexander/New York. Ca. 1937. *Photo by Phyllis Houston. Courtesy Ruby K. Arnold.*

Illustration 263. 13 inch all-composition, fully-jointed "Nurse Doll," carrying no markings. The author is not certain, but this may be the Madame Alexander "Nurse Doll for the Quints." An identical doll is Alexander's "Little Betty." She has the same blue tin sleep eyes, rosebud mouth and blond mohair wig over unpainted, molded hair. She is also unmarked and has the same bent right arm. The dress that the nurse wears is similar to the one in Alexander 1936 advertising for the nurse doll. *Photo by Phyllis Houston. Courtesy Ruby K. Arnold.*

VIII. The Dionne Quintuplet Museum

Right alongside Highway 11 halfway between Callander and North Bay visitors can now see the largest collection of Dionne Quintuplet memorabilia in existence. There are some of the usual calendars, the picture books and cutout books, and other collectibles that sell for a small fortune nowadays. But the museum assemblage is primarily authentic Dionne mementos. The original Dionne farm house in which the Quints were born in 1934 was moved to the main highway in the 1950s as a tourist attraction and sits in Pinewood Park, a motel and golf course complex on Lake Nipissing. The great majority of items in the museum was the belongings of the Dionne family at the time of the Quints' birth and the things that were the girls' as they were growing up.

The Quints Home Museum is the old frame house, spruced up with new paint. It looks much as it did back in 1934. There are three rooms on the first floor—a large kitchen-living room and two bedrooms; upstairs there are three more bedrooms. Originally a "summer kitchen" was attached to the back of the house. It is furnished as it was when the Quints were born. One can see the original bed where Elzire gave birth to the girls; the incubator that saved the babies' lives; the table where the family ate; the wood-burning stove where Mrs. Dionne cooked and on whose oven door the babies were placed in a basket to keep them warm; the mother's sewing machine and all the other furnishings that made up the house. One can at last see, that although the house was modest and it was plain, it was cozy. Even though it lacked many modern conveniences, it was the type of farm house that many a family of similar circumstances in the 1930s would have envied.

The house now belongs to the motor inn and the collection is the property of Mr. and Mrs. Stan Guignard of Callander, who have gathered together the original Dionne possessions and have operated the museum since 1967.

Some of the artifacts acquired by the Guignards include the tiny baby clothes of the Quints, their first communion dresses, the gowns worn by the girls when they were presented to the King and Queen of England, the dresses worn by them on their visit to New York City in 1950, the bridesmaid gowns they wore when they were in their brother Ernest's wedding, their toys and everything else they had during the time they grew up. Mr. Guignard, a friend of the Dionne family, acquired the collection by negotiating personally over the past sixteen years with the family member who had the piece of furniture or other equipment from the original home. All the dresses, baby bottles and toys came from Mrs. Dionne, who had saved them over the years. Everything is in excellent condition.

On the walls are hundreds of framed photographs showing the entire history of the Quints' childhood. The Guignards are also the lucky owners of several of the original oil paintings of the Quintuplets which were used to illustrate the Brown and Bigelow calendars, including "School Days," the picture that shows up in almost every

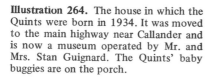

Illustration 264. The house in which the Quints were born in 1934. It was moved to the main highway near Callander and is now a museum operated by Mr. and Mrs. Stan Guignard. The Quints' baby buggies are on the porch.

photograph taken in the "Big House."

Also as part of the collection is a display of Dr. Allan Roy Dafoe's memoirs. There are the utensils used to keep the babies alive in the early days, including the eye droppers from which they were fed the mixture of water and corn syrup. All of the doctor's medical books are there. Even Dafoe's license plates with the lettering D70, a special combination given him by Ontario after the birth of the Quints, are on display.

The museum is a trip into the past, a trip into simpler times and a trip into popular history. It is both amazing to see so many of the belongings of the Dionnes and at the same time it is poignant because of the memories they evoke.

Many of the artifacts are gifts that the Quints received from all over the world, like the silk kimonos sent to them by the Emperor of Japan when they were born. The dolls that the Quints played with and the cradles that they placed them

in are lined up on shelves. There is even a long brown braid of hair from each Quint, which was saved by their mother when their hair was cut short in the 1940s. It is a wonder that so many items were available for the museum.

The Guignards show more hospitality to visitors than is found in most museums and take a personal interest in them. Maintaining and displaying their Dionne Quintuplet collection takes up a major part of their daily lives. Each summer about 15,000 to 20,000 callers sign the guest book that was autographed by such visiting personalities as Clark Gable, Charlie Chaplin and Bette Davis.

Even for those who are not fascinated by the story of the Quints, a visit to the house shows a modern generation a typical wooden walled and ceilinged Canadian farm house of another era. And the Dionne Quintuplets do have their place in history.

Illustration 265. Living room-kitchen of the Dionne home, showing the original furniture that was in the house when the Quints were born and other memorabilia of the girls.

Illustration 266. The bedroom and the bed in which Elzire Dionne gave birth to the Quints. The basket with dolls in it is supposed to be the one in which the babies were placed after birth.

Illustration 267. Wall in the bedroom in which the Quints were born showing pictures, scrapbooks and Christmas cards that they themselves made as children.

Illustration 268. The smaller first-floor bedroom. The baby clothes of the Quints and booklets from their early years are displayed.

Illustration 269. Items used by the Quints and the license plates from Dr. Dafoe's cars.

Illustration 270. On the shelf below the dolls hangs a braid of hair from each Quint tied with a ribbon of her identifying color. The center doll is an 18 inch Shirley Temple.

Illustration 271. Stewart-Warner radio, sold commercially in 1939. On the top and sides of the plastic case there are decals of the Quints in color.

IX. Corbeil Revisited

Today the three surviving Quints, Cécile, Yvonne and Annette, do not come back to Corbeil. Nor do the throngs of tourists. Beautiful Lake Nipissings, with its many islands and thousands of neighboring lakes, is surrounded by thick forests and an unspoiled countryside and is popular with hunters and fishermen. On the lake's eastern shore is North Bay, a modern and progressive city that bills itself as the "Gateway of the North." Callander and Corbeil are close by in this region that is a perfect vacation location, as well as being the entrance to Ontario's rich Northland with its gold, silver, copper and uranium deposits and its vast timber dominions. The highways to Corbeil are even better than they were after they were improved to handle the tourist traffic to "Quintland." But there are no souvenir pavilions, refreshment stands or parking problems. It only takes a few minutes to drive from North Bay to Callander; from Callander to Corbeil even less. Approaching Corbeil, one goes past tall pine trees and substantial rock outcroppings; past the site where the house in which the world's first surviving Quintuplets were born, past the special hospital that was built for them, past the building where the staff who maintained the Quints lived and past the mansion that was built with the money the Quints earned as tourist attractions and commercial commodities.

Corbeil could hardly be called a town. All there is of Corbeil is Sacred Heart Church, where Elzire Legros and Oliva Dionne were married, a school, a post office and a gas station, with a few houses in the outlying area.

A visitor standing at the road sign that names the place Corbeil and looking across the road and back towards Callander would see the remains of the complex that was once Canada's most popular tourist attraction outside of Niagara Falls. A chain-link fence still surrounds "Quintland," behind which the permanent buildings stand yet, in various stages of disrepair. The observation building and the souvenir shacks are long gone.

The Nursery where the Quints stood to sing for the crowds has had the porch removed; a partial second floor has been added; and the present occupant has covered the log paneling with white aluminum siding. It is difficult to imagine that the small house was once the center of world-wide attention and that its occupants captured the imagination of an entire generation.

On the left, next to this private property, is the former dwelling of the nurses and the attendants of Dafoe Hospital. It looks much as it did in the 1930s except that it is now part of a new complex. The fence surrounding this house is the same one protecting Nipissing Manor Nursing Home.

The Manor, once the "Big House" built for the Dionne family, is a "rest home" for the elderly. Being converted to institutional use was the only

Illustration 272. Corbeil, showing Sacred Heart Church.

Illustration 273. Dafoe Hospital, the nursery where the Quints spent their first seven years, now a private home.

salvation for this pretentious structure and the only purposeful use to which such a large home near Corbeil could be realized. There have been modern additions added to the original house to accommodate the hospital facilities of the nursing home. Large dogs, looking like unfriendly wolves, are stationed in kennels near the gate. Warning system? The whole place, including the grounds and the gardens, is half-heartedly maintained. In no way does it strike the observer as a friendly place. The residents are probably no happier than were the former occupants of the mansion. It has the aura of an old-time "madhouse."

Close by this complex is a modern bungalow belonging to a brother of the Quints. And next door is another small brick ranch house with an attached garage. There is nothing fancy or stylish about the house, nothing to signal fame or attention, not even a mailbox with a name on it. There is a Cadillac parked in the driveway though. In this house, only a few hundred yards from the place where the Quints were born in 1934 and just as close to the former Dionne mansion, live Mr. and Mrs. Oliva Dionne in their retirement years.

The Dionnes seek no attention and would not welcome the curious. The fanfare and public notice that brought them only pain and heartbreak is long in the past. (It is interesting though that they built the house on their own property instead of relocating elsewhere.) They live in privacy and in the quiteness that was their way of life before they became famous parents. In this setting they celebratted their 50th wedding anniversary on the 15th of September 1975. The celebration was strictly a family affair and there was no publicity, no photo-

graphers and no outside guests. Oliva Dionne was 72 and Elzire was 66. Joining in the celebration were many of their children, their forty grandchildren and their five great-grandchildren. None of the surviving Quints were present to mark the occasion.

Annette, Yvonne and Cécile remained in Montreal. Marie was buried in St. Bruno. Emilie was buried near Corbeil.

To reach Emilie's grave one has to drive to Corbeil on Highway 64, turn left at the Church, cross the railroad tracks and take the dirt road at the left. About a mile down the narrow lane, lined with high bushes and weeds, past a rundown farm house, one comes to a fenced cow pasture. The gate can be opened and automobiles can safely drive across the pasture with its thin soil over rocky outcroppings. At the end of the pasture is another gate. Beyond this gate is a small cemetery surrounded on two sides by bushes and saplings. At the back of the cemetery, marked by an average size stone, Emilie lies buried alone. Visitors should concentrate on the living, but how many persons ever come to this lonely spot? The author cleaned a hornet's nest of dried mud out of the engraved lettering of her name on the tombstone and reflected on the limitations that time had granted her.

The grave in which Emilie lies, in a lonely place, is symbolic of all the tragedy that befell the Dionne Quintuplets who were born into a world where they were a miracle of Nature and where everyone loved them for a little while and then forgot about them.

Illustration 274. The house where the staff of Dafoe Hospital lived. It is now part of Nipissing Manor Nursing Center.

Illustration 275. Nipissing Manor Nursing Center, the former Dionne mansion with modern additions.

Illustration 276. Nipissing Manor Nursing Center, the "Big House" where the Quints grew up.

Illustration 277. The present home of Mr. and Mrs. Oliva Dionne.

Illustration 278. Elzire and Oliva Dionne for their Golden Wedding Anniversary, September 15, 1975. In the center is their friend, C.M. Fellman, the Managing Editor of the *North Bay Nugget. Courtesy The North Bay Nugget.*

Illustration 279. Pasture field near Corbeil. The cemetery where Emilie is buried is in the background.

Illustration 280. The Corbeil Church cemetery.

Illustration 281. Emilie's grave. To the left is the headstone for the parents of Oliva Dionne. Mr. and Mrs. Legros, the parents of Elzire are buried in front of Emilie.

Pricing Dionne Quintuplet Collectibles

The most nebulous feature of collecting is the price that collectors pay to add to their collection and the price that dealers or others charge them. It is difficult to determine the "fair price" of an item that initially had very little monetary value. Pricing is determined by the availability and the quantity of memorabilia that has been saved, its condition and the eagerness of purchasers to acquire it. The price that a collector should pay is the lowest price possible; the price that a dealer will charge is usually the highest price possible. And if collections are treasured—and loved—they are priceless anyhow.

The "value" of collectibles is determined by their availability and the initial quantity that was produced. Some items are difficult to assign a value to, although these things are advertised in collectors' journals at very high prices. A case in point is the scrapbooks that were compiled so lovingly about 40 years ago. Obviously one made of heavy page stock that included color pictures and magazine covers should be worth more than one that is falling apart because it was a poorly bound scrapbook made of thin paper to begin with, and was compiled with clippings from newspapers showing no dates, no identification and no chronological sequence of presentation. As with many collectibles, the selling price can be unreasonable because of owner sentiment.

The following is a *suggested value* for Dionne Quintuplet collectibles. The first figure is for merchandise that is in fair condition; the second figure is for things that are in excellent condition; the average price falls somewhere in between. Quintuplet-owned items are not considered because of their rarity and their current value. For example, the original oil paintings by Andrew Loomis are presently for sale at $5,000 each.

ADVERTISING booklets with Quint pictures	$2.00. . . . . . $7.00
ADVERTISING page from magazines	$1.00. . . . . . $3.00
Items AUTOGRAPHED by Oliva and/or Elzire Dionne	$7.00. . . . $25.00
BIBS with pictures of the Quints	$4.00. . . . $10.00
Dionne Baby BOOKS	$3.00. . . . $12.00
Dionne Picture BOOKS from the 1930s	$7.00. . . . $15.00
Published BOOKS on the Quints or Dr. Dafoe	$5.00. . . . $10.00
BOOK from University of Toronto Study	$25.00. . . . $50.00
BOOKLETS from advertising with Quint pictures	$2.00. . . . . . $7.00
Dionne picture BOOKLETS with color cover	$2.00. . . . $12.00
Cereal BOWL (chrome-plated)	$6.00. . . . $12.00
BROOCHES, clasps, etc. with picture	$3.00. . . . $10.00
CALENDARS	$2.00. . . . . . $7.00
CATALOGS featuring Quint-endorsed merchandise (The higher figure would reflect the price of a catalog that had Quint items on the cover, and was in *perfect* condition.)	$3.00. . . . $15.00
COVERS of magazines (alone)	$1.00. . . . . . $5.00
Purse CLASPS, brooches, etc.	$3.00. . . . $10.00
CUTOUT DOLLS (See Paper Dolls)	
Toy DISH sets	$8.00. . . . . $30.00
DOLLS	
(The lower figure refers to dolls in fair condition; the higher figure refers to dolls in *like-new* condition that are *all original*.)	

Madame Alexander:

7" Baby	$10.00. . . . $30.00
Complete set of 7" Babies, *not* put-together set	$125.00. . $200.00
Complete set of 7" Babies, *not* put-together set,	

continued page 138

in *original* bed, high chair, merry-go-'round, etc.	$150.00. . $225.00
7½" Toddler with molded hair or wig	$15.00. . . . $40.00
Complete set of 7½" Toddlers, *not* put-together set	$125.00. . $225.00
10" Baby	$15.00. . . . $45.00
11½" Baby	$15.00. . . . $45.00
11½" Toddler with molded hair or wig	$15.00. . . . $40.00
14½" Toddler with molded hair or wig	$15.00. . . . $40.00
16½" Baby	$15.00. . . . $50.00
17" Toddler with molded hair or wig	$20.00. . . . $90.00
17" Girl with wig	$25.00. . . $100.00
17½" Baby	$15.00. . . . $50.00
23" Baby	$20.00. . . . $75.00

NOTE: Complete, *matched* sets of the larger dolls would be valued at about *double* the figure for the price of 5 dolls in the same condition. An original doll box in good condition would add about $15.00 to the price of the doll.

"Dr. Dafoe" Doll	$40.00. . . . $90.00
"Dionne Quint Nurse" doll	$40.00. . . . $80.00
7" plastic and vinyl "Fischer Quint"	$5.00. . . . . $15.00
7" plastic and vinyl boxed set of "Fischer Quints"	$50.00. . . $100.00
EffanBee Baby Tinyettes in *matched* set of five dolls	$70.00. . . $100.00
7" unmarked doll, or *Superior* doll, resembling Alexander or EffanBee 7" sizes	$5.00. . . . . $15.00
All-bisque doll marked Japan in minature sizes	$1.00. . . . . . $5.00
All-bisque doll marked Japan in minature sizes in set of 5 in original box. (Add $5.00 for nurse included.)	$12.00. . . . $30.00
6½" doll of papier-mâché or composition marked Japan, resembling Alexander Dionne dolls	$5.00. . . . . $15.00
FANS	$3.00. . . . . $10.00
FERTILITY stones or rocks (see stones)	
Individual doll FURNITURE from "Dionne Quintuplet's Home"	$10.00. . . . $25.00
GAMES, puzzles, etc.	$5.00. . . . . $12.00
HANDKERCHIEFS	$2.00. . . . . . $8.00
"Dionne Quintuplet's HOME" from Madame Alexander, including 5 Quint dolls, nurse doll, 5 pieces of wooden furniture	$500.00. $1500.00
China LAMPS	$20.00. . . . $50.00
Original LETTERS from Dr. Dafoe	$25.00. . . . $50.00
Complete MAGAZINES	
Quints on Cover. (General magazines would be valued less; The Shirley Temple cover of *Modern Screen*, i.e., would carry the higher value)	$3.00. . . . . $25.00
Quints featured in articles and pictures	$2.00. . . . . . $7.00
Quints featured in advertising	$2.00. . . . . . $5.00
MAGAZINE covers (alone)	$1.00. . . . . . $5.00
MAGAZINE page or article	$1.00. . . . . . $3.00
Pressed MEDALS, made from pennies	. . . . $5.00
Pathegrams MOVIE films	$20.00. . . $100.00
Sheet MUSIC	$2.00. . . . . . $6.00
NEWSPAPERS (in good condition)	?
Clippings with no dates, no titles	
Entire pages with *feature* articles and/or photos	$1.00. . . . . . $3.00
Front Page with article and/or photos	. . . . $4.00
Front Page with headlines	$5.00. . . . . $10.00
Front Page from May 1934 with Quint Birth	

Continued page 139

Article and/or pictures	$10.00.... $30.00
North Bay Nugget Special "Quintuplet Edition" (complete)	.... $10.00
Sunday Rotogravure sections with at least one page of photographs	.... $5.00
PAGE of advertising from magazines	$1.00...... $3.00
PAPER DOLLS	
Sets that are cut out	$5.00.... $16.00
Un-cut booklets	$7.00.... $20.00
Booklets of Quintuplets printed after 1964	$2.00...... $4.00
PENNANTS from the 1940s	$2.00...... $5.00
Original PHOTOGRAPHS and *original* "stills" from movies	$1.00...... $4.00
Framed souvenir PHOTOGRAPHS from "Quintland"	$3.00.... $25.00
China PLATES	$10.00.... $40.00
PLAYING CARDS (complete decks, boxed)	$10.00.... $20.00
Quaker Oats PORTRAITS	$1.00...... $4.00
Original POSTCARDS from "Quintland" before 1940	$1.00...... $2.00
PUZZLES, games, etc.	$5.00..... $12.00
Stewart-Warner RADIO (complete)	$35.00... $150.00
Hair RIBBONS on card	$3.00...... $8.00
Hair RIBBON in brooch clasp, showing Quints	$5.00..... $12.00
SCRAPBOOK	
The price would be determined by	?
condition, content, presentation, etc.	
SHEET MUSIC	$2.00...... $6.00
SOUVENIRS of Callander, depicting the Quints	$7.00..... $20.00
Authentic SOUVENIRS from stands in "Quintland" (minature spoons, etc., not marked Dionne)	$1.00...... $6.00
SPOONS	
individual spoons	$3.00..... $10.00
complete sets—*not* put-together set; matched for wear, etc.	$25.00.... $60.00
Quint STICKERS for car windows from the 1940s	$1.00...... $3.00
Original movie "STILLS"	$1.00...... $4.00
Authenticated "FERTILITY STONES" purchased from Oliva Dionne before 1940	.... $25.00
TRAVEL literature featuring the Quints	$1.00...... $5.00

NOTE: Items that are not listed, such as: tablets, coloring books, etc., would be priced according to items in similar categories.

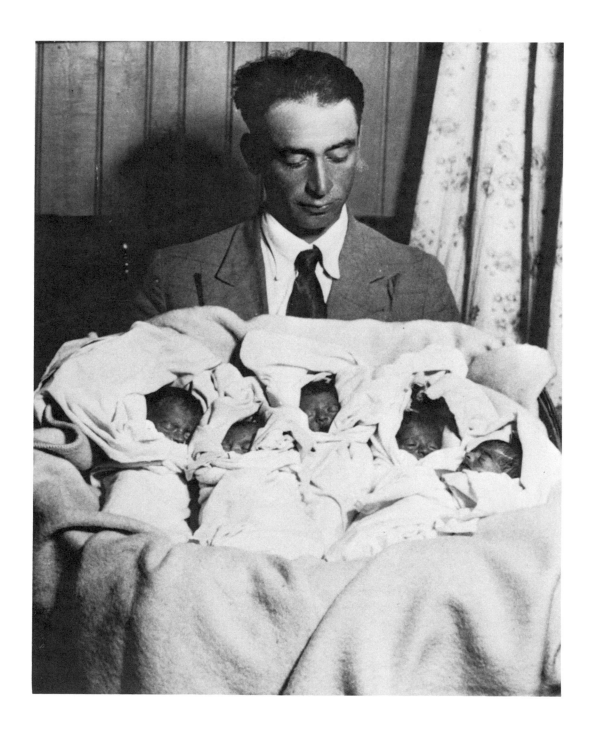

Bibliography

Books

Barker, Lillian. *The Dionne Legend: Quintuplets in Captivity*. New York: Doubleday and Co., Inc., 1951.

Barker, Lillian. *The Quints Have a Family*. New York: Sheed & Ward, 1941.

Brough, James. With Annette, Cécile, Marie and Yvonne Dionne. *We Were Five: The Dionne Quintuplets' Story From Birth Through Childhood To Womanhood*. New York: Simon and Schuster, 1965.

Hunt, Frazier. *The Little Doc: The Story of Allan Roy Dafoe, Physician to the Quintuplets*. New York: Simon and Schuster, 1939.

St. George's School for Child Study. *Collected Studies on the Dionne Quintuplets*. Canada: The University of Toronto Press, 1937.

Newspapers of the Period

Cleveland News
The Enquirer and Evening News (Battle Creek)
The Erie Daily Times
The Globe and Mail (Toronto)
The New York Times
The North Bay Nugget
The Pittsburgh Press
The Repository (Canton, Ohio)
The Sault Daily Star (Sault Ste. Marie, Ontario)
The Star (Toronto)
The Toronto Telegram
The Youngstown Telegram
The Younstown Vindicator

Periodicals

American Magazine
September	1934	
March	1937	What 5 Babies Did to a Town
November	1937	Karo page ad (color)
April	1952	I Had a Date with the Quints

Better Homes and Gardens
September	1935	Five of a Kind
September	1937	Moulding the Quints
January	1938	Scientists of a Continent Discuss the Quints
February	1938	Mrs. Schultz Visits the Quints

Canadian Forum
| May | 1936 | The Government and the Quints |

Capper's Farmer
| February | 1938 | Karo page ad |

Click
| June | 1940 | Cover |
| | | *Click* Visits the Dionne Quints |

Collier's
| April 23, | 1949 | The Strange Case of the Dionne Quints |
| May 27, | 1950 | Birth of the Quints: The Untold Story |

Commonwealth
| July 24, | 1936 | |

Cosmopolitan

March	1936	Separate the Quints

Country Gentleman

March	1938	Karo page ad

Country Home

April	1938	Karo page ad
November	1939	Karo ad

Family Circle

December	25, 1936	review of "Reunion"
January	27, 1939	Karo ad (b&w)
September	18, 1942	The Quints Go Home

Farmer's Wife

September	1934	Electrolux page ad
December	1936	Quints Toy Tea Set premium offer
September	1937	Palmolive page ad (color)
December	1937	Karo page ad (color)

Fortune

December	1936	dolls

Forum

October	1934	

Good Housekeeping

February	1937	Palmolive page ad (color)
		Karo page ad (color)
		Colgate ad
		Quaker Oats ad
June	1937	Palmolive page ad (color)
		Colgate ad
		Lysol ad
September	1937	Palmolive page ad (color)
December	1937	Hinds ad
		Colgate ad
		Quaker Oats ad
December	1938	Karo page ad (color)
March	1939	Karo page ad (color)
June	1939	Palmolive ad
October	1940	Sanitized mattress ad
November	1940	Karo page ad (color) Yvonne portrait
		Sanitized mattress ad
May	1941	Sanitized mattress ad

Harpers

November	1938	Infant Industry: The Quintuplets

Hollywood

March	1936	Meet the Quints
November	1936	The Movie Future of the Quints
August	1937	Palmolive page ad (color)
December	1938	Santa Sometimes Rings Twice
February	1939	Karo page ad (color)
April	1939	Karo page ad (color)
August	1939	Come to the Quintuplets Birthday Party

Household

February	1937	Karo page ad (color)
		Palmolive page ad (color)
		Colgate page ad

Household (continued)

	February	1938	Karo page ad (color)

Hygeia

	February	1936	

Ladies Home Journal

July	1936	Lysol page ad
February	1940	
April	1940	What to Do if Baby is Premature
June	1974	The Dionne Quints at 40

Liberty

June	29, 1935	Private Life of the Dionne Quints
June	6, 1936	Cover
		How the Quintuplets Are Getting Rich
November	14, 1936	I Am the Most Unhappy Mother in the World
		Picture on movie page from "Reunion"
July	9, 1938	Jackie Coogan and the Quints
September	3, 1938	What's Ahead For the Five?
January	27, 1940	The 5 Unbelieved Children in the World
May	11, 1940	What Does the Future Hold for the Quints?
May	29, 1941	Cover
		How the Quints Are Growing Up
April	26, 1941	Baby Ruth ad
October	4, 1941	Cover
		Baby Ruth ad
December	6, 1941	The Quints and the Kidnappers
Summer	1975	Private Life of the Dionne Quints (reprint)

Life

February	15, 1936	News picture in Zanuck article
May	17, 1937	Cover
		Quints Round Out First 3 Years
October	11, 1937	*Life* Reports on the Quints
December	27, 1937	Christmas in Quintupletland
January	17, 1938	Quint Look-Alike
January	16, 1939	The Five Sisters
January	15, 1940	Marie Loses Tooth
September	2, 1940	Cover
		They Enter the age of Reason
December	9, 1940	Kre-Mel page ad (color)
December	30, 1940	Calendar Art
May	19, 1941	Quint Look-Alike
December	29, 1941	*Life* Goes to the Dionnes' Christmas Party
March	6, 1944	Super Twins
January	1, 1945	Calendars
April	21, 1947	Quints as Bridesmaids
September	12, 1949	*Life* Congratulates...Rose Marie Dionne
November	13, 1950	What the Quints Saw in New York
June	16, 1952	The Quints Are 18
November	16, 1953	A Veil for Marie
August	16, 1954	Death of Emilie
August	23, 1954	The Famous Five Are Now Four
April	8, 1957	First of the Quints to Say 'Mai Oui'
May	19, 1972	35 Years Ago

Literary Digest

May	25, 1935	The Dionnes and How They Grew
December	14, 1935	On the Current Screen ("The Country Doctor")
March	14, 1936	Review of "The Country Doctor"
May	16, 1936	Hardy Quintuplets
August	22, 1936	Quintupling Assets

Look
April	26,	1938	
May	24,	1938	How the Quintuplets Differ From Each Other
June	7,	1938	Cover
			Quints Fourth Birthday
August	2,	1938	How You Can See All 14 Dionnes Together
October	11,	1938	Cover
November 8,		1938	Latest News of the Quints
November 22,		1938	How Would You Rear the Quints?
February	14,	1939	Yvonne is Voted Prettiest Quint
			Karo ad
June	17,	1952	Now They Are 18

MacLean's Magazine
July	15,	1941	The Quint Question
June	1,	1944	The Quints Retire
December	15,	1950	My Neighbors The Quints

McCall's
June	1936	So You're Going to See the Quintuplets
October	1936	Quaker Oats ad
May	1938	Heredity or Environment
October	1963	We Were Five
November	1963	We Were Five (cont'd.)
February	1964	Four Dionnes Write and Open Letter to Five Fischers

Modern Screen
March	1936	Lights! Camera! It's the Quints!
April	1936	Cover
		Off Screen Glimpse of the Quints
		Lysol page ad
		Alexander Quint doll ad
July	1936	Cover
		How Much Money Have the Quints?
April	1937	Cover
		I Want to Play with the Quints
		Karo page ad (color)
September	1937	Palmolive page ad (color)
December	1937	Karo page ad (color)
		Hinds ad
February	1938	Karo page ad (color)
March	1938	Karo page ad (color)
October	1938	Karo page ad (color)
June	1939	Palmolive ad

Motion Picture
March	1936	The Quints Become Movie Stars
May	1936	Review and pictures of "The Country Doctor"
November	1936	The Quints Talk
December	1936	Romantic Movie Stories ad
		"Reunion" ad
February	1937	"Reunion" pictures and review
April	1939	Karo page ad (color)

Movie Classic
March	1936	A 5 Star Picture and the Quints Are In It
April	1936	Little Quints You've Had a Busy Day

Movie Mirror
March	1936	Movie Diary of the Quints
		Lysol page ad

Movie Mirror (continued)

September	1936	The Dionne Quints and Their Movie Money
December	1936	"Reunion" page ad
January	1937	Day by Day with the Quints
February	1937	Karo page ad (color)
August	1937	Karo page ad (color)
February	1938	Karo page ad (color)
April	1938	Karo page ad (color)
November	1938	Karo page ad (color)
February	1939	Karo page ad (color)

Movie Story

February	1939	Karo page ad (color)
April	1939	Karo page ad (color)
June	1939	Palmolive ad

Nation

June	19,	1935	The Quintuplets Entertain

National Geographic Magazine, The

February	1935	Old France in Modern Canada
April	1940	Fisher Body ad (color)

Newsweek

June	9,	1934	
August	18,	1934	
March	23,	1935	Ontario Adopts Five World Famous Little Girls
May	25,	1935	Dionnes
May	29,	1937	
June	5,	1939	Dionne Squabbles
May	29,	1944	Cover
			The Quints Mark a Decade
November	27,	1944	Five Minds of Their Own
October	30,	1950	
August	16,	1954	Four Are Left
June	6,	1955	Million-Dollar Birthday
January	9,	1956	The Unhappy Dionnes

New York Times Magazine

June	24,	1934	Feature Article
May	26,	1940	Feature Article
May	28,	1944	Feature Article

Nostalgia Illustrated

February	1975	The Dionne Quintuplets

Parents' Magazine

October	1935	Cover
May	1936	The Private Life of the Quintuplets
		"The Country Doctor"
January	1937	My Visit to the Quintuplets
February	1937	Dr. Dafoe Himself
		Karo page ad (color)
		Colgate page ad
		Quaker Oats ad
April	1938	Karo page ad (color)
May	1938	Now the Five Are Four
January	1939	Doll premium
April	1939	Karo page ad (color)
October	1939	Carnation milk ad
December	1939	Baby Ruth ad

May		1941	Baby Ruth ad
June		1942	What the Quintuplets Like To Eat

Pathfinder

February	27,	1946	Picture of Quints with Snow Queen

Photoplay

March	1936	How They Got the Quints in Pictures
December	1936	The Dionne Quints in Pictures "Reunion" page ad
January	1937	Pictures and reviews of "Reunion"
November	1938	
February	1941	Karo page ad (color) Marie

Physical Culture

January	1937	The Adorable Quints Again
March	1937	Karo page ad (color)

Pictorial Review

May	1935	What About the Other Five Dionnes?
September	1936	The Dionne Quints Twenty Years From Today
December	1937	Karo ad (color)

Picture Play

November	1938	Amazing Change in the Quints
December	1938	"Five of a Kind"

Popular Photography

January	1938	Picture of Quints in film ad

Popular Science

February	1937	Photographing the Dionne Quins

Radio Guide

April	18,	1936	Will They Be Radio Stars Tomorrow?
April	25,	1936	Will They Be Radio Stars Tomorrow?
June	13,	1936	Baby Talk

Reader's Digest

November	1936	Canadian Mecca
December	1938	Infant Industry
January	1950	My Life with the Dionne Quintuplets

Recreation

July	1942	
October	1945	A Queen's Life is Boring

Redbook

April	1955	What's Ahead For the Quints?
May	1955	What's Ahead For the Quints?
October	1961	The Quints and Their 7 Children

Romantic Movie Stars

December	1936	Quint Contest "Reunion"

Rotarian

April	1942	What the Quints Have Taught Me

Saturday Evening Post
April   23, 1938
May   14, 1938   Little Doc
May   21, 1938   Little Doc
May   28, 1938   Little Doc

Saturday Night
May   6, 1944   Quietus on the Quints, or the Famous Five
                                go Un-famous
October   20, 1951   Dionne Legend

School Life
December   1937   Quintuplets Discussed

Scientific News Letter
November 13, 1937   Why Do the Quints Differ? A Puzzle for Science
June   4, 1938   Quints Identical, Patterns of Finger Base Indicate

Screen Album
Fall   1936   Page of pictures

Screen Book
March   1936   Stardom For the Quints!
May   1936   "Country Doctor" review and pictures
December   1939   Karo 1/2-page ad (color)

Screen Guide
June   1936   Things You Never Knew Before About the Quints
December   1936   The Unknown Life of the Quints by
                                Rochelle Hudson

Screenland
March   1936   The Quintuplets Are Movie Stars Now
December   1936   "Reunion" page ad

Screenplay
May   1936   Will They Separate the Quints?
November   1936   Quints' First Interview

Screen Romances
April   1936   The Country Doctor
December   1938   Cover
                                Five of a Kind

Silver Screen
March   1936   Lysol page ad
May   1936   "The Country Doctor" pictures and review
December   1936   "Reunion" page ad
September   1938   On Location With the Quints

Song Hits
December   1938   Lyrics from "Five of a Kind"

Stage
December   1935   Musical Quintesence (Quintuplet Lullaby)

Standard Magazine
March   21, 1942   Callander Tragedy

Successful Farming
September   1935   5 Little Farm Girls
April   1938   Karo page ad (color)

Time

June	11,	1934	Quintuplets
March	16,	1936	"The Country Doctor" review
December	7,	1936	"Reunion" review
May	31,	1937	Cover
			The Quints and How They Grew
November	8,	1937	Y-A-C-E-M
October	31,	1938	"Five of a Kind" review
March	22,	1944	
June	3,	1946	Five Turned Twelve
May	31,	1948	Birthday picture
August	16,	1954	Late But Inexorable
January	9,	1956	Life Without Father

Time (Canadian Edition)

October	9,	1950	Finery For Five

True Story

June	1936	Quints Nurse Tells Story of Dionnes
February	1939	Whose Children Are the Quintuplets (Papa Dionne)
		A Distinguished Canadian Replies to Papa Dionne
		Karo page ad (color)

Weekly Illustrated (British)

May	4, 1935	The Quins Are Teething

Woman's Home Companion

August	1935	Cover
		A Squint at the Quints
		Lysol page ad
February	1937	Karo page ad (color)
		Palmolive page ad (color)
		Colgate page ad
		Quaker Oats ad
May	1937	Karo page ad (color)
		Colgate page ad
		Quaker Oats ad
June	1939	Making Movies With the World's Most Famous Sisters

Woman's World

November	1936	The Quints
March	1937	Palmolive page ad (color)
May	1937	Palmolive page ad (color)
August	1937	Palmolive page ad (color)

Index

Index of Dionne Quintuplet Collectibles appears after the General Index.
Bold-face type refers to Illustration numbers, not page numbers.

Index of Dionne Quintuplet Collectibles

PHOTO CREDITS:

Author, **50A, 51, 56, 70, 72A-73D, 74-151, 153-154, 161-162, 168-170, 172-261, 264, 272-277**

C. Kenneth Clark, Jr., **265-271, 279-281**

Phyllis Houston, **262-263**

International News Photo/King Features, **34-38, 40-45**

North Bay Nugget, **278**

Fay Rodolfos, **71A, 73E**

Paul Zimmerman, **152**

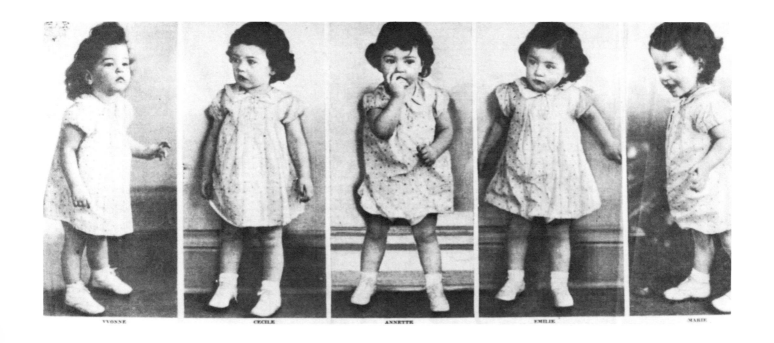

154